Secrets of God's Armor

The Weapons of Righteousness Series

Gil Stieglitz

Secrets of God's Armor
Weapons of Righteousness Series
Building Strong Christians for the Battle

© 2015 Gil Stieglitz

Published by Principles to Live By, Roseville CA 95661
www.ptlb.com

Cover by John Chase
Copyedited by Jennifer Edwards and Sandy Johnson

All rights reserved. No part of this publication may be reproduced, stored in a retrieval system, or transmitted in any way by an means-electronic, mechanical, photocopy, recording, or otherwise-without the prior permission of the copyright holder, except as provided by USA copyright law.

Scripture verses are from the New American Standard Bible unless otherwise indicated.
New American Standard Bible: 1995 update.
1995 La Habra, CA: The Lockman Foundation.

ISBN 978-0-9909641-1-7
Christian Living

Printed in the United States of America

Table of Contents

Introduction...5
Chapter 1 - Overall Resistance................................. 15
Chapter 2 - Spiritual Weapon of Truth......................... 19
Chapter 3 - Spiritual Weapon of Righteousness.............. 53
Chapter 4 - Spiritual Weapon of Peace......................... 87
Chapter 5 - Spiritual Weapon of Faith....................... 113
Chapter 6 - Spiritual Weapon of Salvation.................. 131
Chapter 7 - Spiritual Weapon of the Word of God.......... 151
Chapter 8 - Spiritual Weapon of Prayer...................... 169
Chapter 9 - Spiritual Weapon of Alertness.................. 195
Chapter 10 - Building the Hedge of Protection.............. 213
Chapter 11 - Overview of the Armor of God................ 221
Conclusion... 225
How to Use This Book.. 233
About the Author.. 241
Other Resources... 243

Secrets of God's Armor
Introduction

The goal of the Christian life is NOT to battle Satan. The goal of the Christian life is to love God, love others, and righteously love yourself (Matthew 22:37,38). In order to build a dynamic, hilarious, enjoyable life full of love for God and others you will have to battle Satan in many forms. You may face Satan as bitterness over the injustice that will happen to you. You may face Satan as the anger that wants to punish others every time you don't get your way. You may face Satan as the fear that grips your whole being and tries to have you pull back into a small, little life. You may face Satan as invitations to give yourself to occultic spiritual power to gain safety, security, or something else you want. You may face Satan through the constant thoughts that "It is all about me." But the focus should not be on battling Satan but on the positive life of love that God wants you to build. It is only in building with God a positive life of love that everyone wins. God has given us powerful spiritual weapons to help us carve out this enjoyable life of love. These are called in Scripture the Armor of God. They are practical weapons that really do work in creating a life of love. Unfortunately many times these spiritual weapons have been over-theologized and over-analyzed to the point where no one practically knows how to use them. Look at Ephesians 6:10-18:

> *Finally, be strong in the Lord and in the strength of His might. Put on the full armor of God, so that you will be able to stand firm against the schemes of the devil. For our struggle is not against flesh and blood, but against*

the rulers, against the powers, against the world forces of this darkness, against the spiritual forces of wickedness in the heavenly places. Therefore, take up the full armor of God, so that you will be able to resist in the evil day, and having done everything, to stand firm. Stand firm therefore, HAVING GIRDED YOUR LOINS WITH TRUTH, and HAVING PUT ON THE BREASTPLATE OF RIGHTEOUSNESS, and having shod YOUR FEET WITH THE PREPARATION OF THE GOSPEL OF PEACE; in addition to all, taking up the shield of faith with which you will be able to extinguish all the flaming arrows of the evil one. And take THE HELMET OF SALVATION, and the sword of the Spirit, which is the word of God. With all prayer and petition pray at all times in the Spirit, and with this in view, be on the alert with all perseverance and petition for all the saints.

This book is an attempt to bring these weapons back to their practical use and to correct the distortions and misapplications of these verses. These weapons are **Truth, Righteousness, Peace, Faith, Ways of Escape, The Word of God, Prayer, and Alertness**. God is right now bringing these weapons to you to use in the building of your abundant life of love. These weapons cut through the lies, fear, doubt, despair, bondage, traps, hatred, myths, bitterness, anger, and stupidity that the Devil is selling you.

God does not give us theories in Scripture. He tells us how to live in a dynamic and restful way (Matthew 11:28-30). Sometimes preachers and teachers have covered over what the Bible says very plainly, and we miss what God is really saying to us. Unfortunately, this tendency to produce unhelpful analysis is at a zenith in the area of spiritual warfare and the use of the Armor of God. So many of the explanations of the Armor of God

Introduction

over-analyze the Roman military hardware and obscure the obvious spiritual weapon.

Rather than repeat the exegetical analysis and theological presuppositions that have rendered the Armor of God practically useless, I was prompted to begin with a different biblical starting place and a different biblical data set for analysis. Spiritual warfare is about how godly people pushed back the Devil and built a life of love and joy in the midst of temptations, testing, and pain. I was prompted to look at every encounter in the Scripture that godly men and women had with Satan—all the way from Job, to Moses, to other Old Testament saints, to Jesus, to the apostles, and to the believers in Revelation. What I found was astonishing. The heroes of the faith (including the Lord himself) did not approach the problem of spiritual warfare the way that many teachers of our day suggest. What we see in the Scriptures is that the heroes of the faith consistently used one or more of the weapons that the Apostle Paul calls the Armor of God (Truth, Righteousness, Peace, Faith, Ways of Escape, the Word of God, Prayer, and Alertness) in very practical ways. Unfortunately in many instances we don't understand them, don't know how to use them, or aren't practiced in the art of using them against the Devil.

The heroes of the faith used the spiritual weapons - God's Armor - in a very straightforward manner:

- They spoke truth at the Devil's lies.
- They acted righteously in the face of the Devil's temptations.
- They made peace with God and others rather than participate in strife, anger, and/or violence.
- They trusted God and took risks to build a greater life of love for God, others or themselves while the Devil sought to confuse them, make them feel alone, and get them to play it safe without the risks inherent in love.

- They looked for and embraced every one of God's ways of escape knowing that He would provide them with one when the Devil attacked or tried to trap them.
- They listened for the whispers of God bringing Scripture for the decisions they were facing countering the Devil's logic and seductions.
- They prayed to God in multiple formats and multiple ways asking that they be allowed to build a life of love as the Devil pushed on them to give up and give in to the hopelessness he was selling.
- They stayed alert to the feedback God was giving them and prepared for the ways the Devil could come after them in the future.

Everything the heroes of the faith did to ward off the Devil was built on the foundation of proper theology but notice that we do not see them making long, theological diatribes at the Devil. In fact, theology isn't one of the weapons in the victory! Rather, theology is behind the victory; it undergirds the victory. Correct biblical theology is the "why" behind how these weapons work, but it is the weapons themselves that win the victory. We see the heroes of the faith thrusting truth, righteous actions, strategies of peace, God-designed risk, daring ways of escape, whispers of God's Word, specific prayers, and alertness to feedback in to the face of the Devil. And they won over and over again with these simple but powerful spiritual weapons. The Devil does not want to see the believer become proficient in using these weapons for they spell his doom. Therefore, the Devil tries to hide the truth of these weapons.

At the end of each chapter we will walk through a number of very simple but practical ways of using these spiritual weapons. We will also show you some of the verses detailing how the heroes of the faith used each one. The strategies we want you to

Introduction

learn are how to practically use these weapons to build an abundant life of love.

The Armor of God is one of the greatest weapons systems in our struggle against the Devil. When you face times and seasons of intense emotion, temptation, or evil ideas, strap on the spiritual armor that God has provided. All together the Armor of God is a series of pieces that form a spiritual force field.

The eight spiritual weapons develop a force-field around the Christian

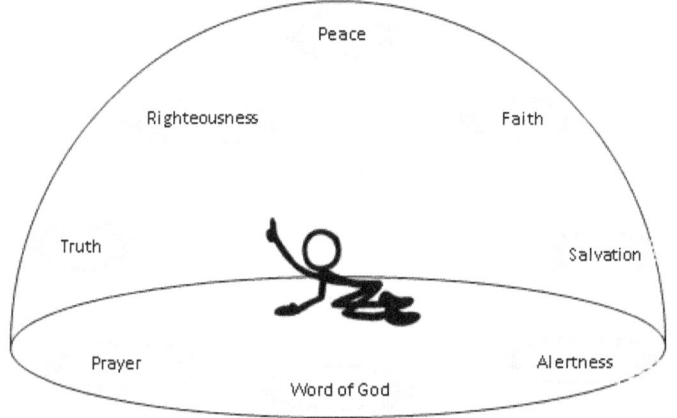

The Apostle Paul was in a Roman prison when he penned the words in Ephesians 6. His purpose is to prepare and strengthen Christians in their actual battles with the Devil. God has given the Christian believer eight specific spiritual weapons to resist demonic pressure (Truth, Righteousness, Peace, Faith, Ways of Escape, The Word of God, Prayer, and Alertness). He wants Christians to realize that these are not concepts, ideas, or nice qualities; but rather they are powerful, practical, spiritual weapons. Indeed they are as practical to the spiritual war as military armor is to the soldier. Christians need spiritual protection and offensive weaponry. God has provided it through these eight weapons. Together they form the basic weapons system for battling the Devil to build a God-honoring life.

Writing under the inspiration of God's Holy Spirit, the Apostle Paul connects six of these spiritual weapons with a piece of armor that Roman soldiers wore (Truth, Righteousness, the Gospel of Peace, Faith, Salvation, the Word of God). This connection to Roman military armor allows people to remember the spiritual weapons more easily. The last two spiritual weapons do not have a Roman military counterpart, so Paul just mentions them as essential spiritual weapons (prayer and alertness). The spiritual weapons are invisible but using metaphors of Roman armor, they can be made visible to us. The illustration of Roman armor powerfully helps us see the battle and the weapons. But remember, these spiritual weapons do far more than the Roman pieces did.

There is a subtle danger in associating the spiritual armor with the Roman armor. We can believe that the spiritual weapon will act in the same way and with the same limitations as the Roman pieces of armor. Each of the spiritual pieces of armor is spiritually powerful way beyond any comparison to belts, shields, swords, and the like. Truth devastates lies and sets people free from the superstitions and fears of their past. A belt doesn't do that. Righteous actions change the course of history, bless others, build loving relationships, and echoes through our lives. A breastplate doesn't do that. God making peace with us and commissioning us to be peacemakers with His strategies transforms individuals, families, communities, and even nations. Sandals don't do that. God-designed risks push us to new levels of achievement, push back oppression, stop injustice, gather people for righteous purposes, and spread love when only hate has displayed itself. A wooden, cloth, or metal shield doesn't do that. God's willingness to send His Son Jesus Christ to die for us so He could offer a way of escape from the wrath of God has changed everything about the spiritual world and our relationship with God. To equate that incredible spiritual power to a leather or metal helmet too closely diminishes our use of and understanding of Christ's salvation. When God whispers just the right words from His book into our soul in the midst of a battle with temptation, fear, or doubt, we feel the power and wisdom of God. A small Roman sword can't do what God speaking His Word can do.

God has used the analogy of the Roman armor to teach us that we are in a spiritual battle and that these spiritual weapons should be ready for action at all times. But the spiritual weapons are in another league of weaponry. Unfortunately many Christians spend too much time studying Roman military weaponry rather than the actual spiritual weapons God mentions in this passage. It is the spiritual weapons that will bring victory, not the Roman equipment. We are facing a spiritual enemy, not a physical enemy. God tells us to employ these eight weapons to resist spiritual attack. We are not putting on an actual belt, but we are injecting truth into our minds. We are not strapping on a breastplate, but we are acting righteously ourselves empowered by and because of Christ's righteousness. We are not lacing up sandals, but we are making peace with God, others, and ourselves because of Christ's accomplishment of peace with God for us. We are not holding up a wooden shield against a physical enemy, but we are taking Christ - honoring risks, trusting Him to guide us through our present difficulty. We are not slipping on a helmet, but we are looking for God's ways of escape if we have been trapped or tempted by the Devil. We are not swinging a physical sword, but we are listening for God's Word whispered in our soul and quoting (quietly or loudly) the Scriptures that pertain to the pressure we are facing.

There were no Roman military counterparts to prayer or alertness, so God just had the Apostle Paul tell us about these spiritual weapons without imagery. We cannot erect the full force field without these last two spiritual weapons. If this Scripture were written in modern times, Paul might have said the "phone call of prayer." The real point is that interaction with God (prayer) is vital for resisting the Devil's pressure. In the intense time of spiritual battle, we must be able to pray in multiple ways to advance our life of love and be protected on the backside.

God has also given us the spiritual weapon called alertness (we call it feedback or warning systems) in order to make us spiritually sensitive to a person, a program, a book, an idea, or an opportunity that is just not right. Again, if this Scripture had been written in our modern era, he might have written about the "radar of alertness" or "the feedback loop." We must be spiritually alert to the schemes of the Devil. Remember, God wants us to build a wonderful life full of love for God, others, and righteously for ourselves. The Devil is doing all he can to block that from happening.

The weapons are divided into two types: those that must always be worn by the believer (Truth, Righteousness, and Strategies of Peace) and those that need to be picked up at a moment's notice for a specific altercation (Faith, Salvation, Word of God, Prayer, and Alertness). The Christian should be familiar with using these spiritual weapons. God gave us all of these so that we can resist the pressure of the Devil in whatever form he comes at us and build a great life of love. We are to stand firm for what is right. We are not to be moved from righteousness, love, and joy by the Devil's trickery. Satan will do all manner of things so that it will seem like we need to be full of hate, resentment, cynicism, or be OK with ignoring moral boundaries.

Introduction

Spiritual Workout

Practical Prayer through the eight pieces of Armor

Which one of the following spiritual weapons is God prompting you to use this week?

Truth
Righteous Actions
Harmony /Peace Strategies
Risk / Trust
Ways of Escape/ Deliverance
Biblical Words & Thoughts
Specific Prayers
Feedback / Warning Systems

Pray slowly through the list of spiritual weapons called the Armor of God. Which one or two is God highlighting? We have become convinced that these weapons are so complex that we can't begin using them without years of training. No, they are simple weapons. There are many ways to learn to use them but start using them. God wants you to use these spiritual weapons to cut through the lies, manipulation, and deception of the Devil. One or two of these weapons are the key to making progress toward the life that God wants you to have. You are only a few righteous choices away from a much better life.

Ask God to show you how to use this weapon in the next few days. Be on the lookout for practical ways to utilize this spiritual energy to create a better future. Become familiar with this list and pray through it often. When you encounter crisis or difficulties, one of these spiritual tools will often be the way through the problem.

Yes, there are deep theological truths that undergird these spiritual weapons, but they are meant to be used by regular folks.

Cut through lies, myths, and fables of the world with truth. Beat back temptation through opposite righteous actions. Be a peacemaker rather than a selfish destructive force in your relationships. Break out of the Devil's shallow sinful choices by taking righteous risks. When the tests or the temptations are overwhelming, look for and take God's way of salvation. Meditate on specific verses from the Bible for direction and wisdom rather than the slogans and mantras of the world. Ask God to fulfill your righteous dreams so you can be seeing God work on your behalf. Listen to God's warnings instead of ignoring them and being trapped in sin or a damaged relationship.

Chapter 1
Overall Resistance

Resistance is the key overall strategy that the apostles consistently say to use when you encounter the Devil. In the following scriptures each of the apostles specifically uses the word **RESIST** when they talk about what to do when the Devil attacks us. This is not a coincidence. Prepare to resist.

> *Therefore, take up the full armor of God, so that you will be able **to resist** in the evil day, and having done everything, to stand firm.*
> Ephesians 6:13

> *Be of sober spirit, be on the alert. Your adversary, the devil, prowls around like a roaring lion, seeking someone to devour. But **resist** him, firm in your faith, knowing that the same experiences of suffering are being accomplished by your brethren who are in the world.* 1 Peter 5:8,9

> *Submit therefore to God. **Resist the devil** and he will flee from you. Draw near to God and He will draw near to you.* James 4:7,8a

What does resistance look like?

If the Devil is for something, you are to be against it. He is for the things that would harm you or cause you to stumble into sin. So if he wants you to get the promotion, then you don't want it. If he is pushing you into a relationship, then you move away from that relationship. If he is trying to paralyze you with fear, then you move ahead through the fear to God's goal. If he is filling your head with doubt, then you get the answers you need and choose to move forward with new confidence. If he surrounds you with depression and suicidal thoughts, then you move toward purpose and your significant contributions. If he wants you to wreck your finances through debt and wild spending, then it is time to head in the opposite direction and be responsible in your money management and strategic generosity. Sometimes you don't make much progress when Satan is launching a withering attack but standing your ground is success. Other times he is trying to drive you in one direction, and you can resist him by heading in the opposite direction.

Spiritual Workout

The most powerful use of each weapon

Each of the pieces of the Armor of God are powerflul weapons for building the life you want and resisting the pressure from the Devil. In many cases the path to the life that is the best for you is blocked or you are on the wrong path. These weapons will reorient your life or get you unstuck or help you eliminate the destructive choices you are making now. Let's begin the process of using these weapons by praying through the list of weapons and asking God for just one answer.

What is the one use of this piece of the Armor of God that would make the most difference?

Slowly pray through each spiritual weapon asking God to help you understand the one most powerful use of that weapon right now in your life. Write it down and ask God to guide you to the use of that weapon today and this next week. These spiritual weapons are supposed to be used. You will discover many ways to use these weapons in the weeks ahead, but this is a dynamic place to start.

Key Truths

What is the most powerful truth or use of truth for my life right now?

Righteous Actions

What is the most powerful righteous action I can do in my life right now?

Harmony /Peace Strategies

What is the most powerful peace or harmony strategy that I can use in my life right now?

Risk / Trust

What is the most righteous risk that I can take right now in my life?

Ways of Escape/ Deliverance

What righteous way of escape do I need to take right now in my life?

Biblical Words & Thoughts

What is the most powerful verse that I should be thinking about right now?

Specific Prayers

What are the most important things I should be praying about right now?

Warning Systems

What is the most important warning that I should be paying attention to right now?

Chapter #2
Spiritual Weapon of Truth

The Devil is fundamentally trying to deceive us. He is doing all he can to deprive us of the truth we need to accomplish God's will. The first piece of God's Armor is Truth. Let that sink in. One of the premier ways to fight the Devil is to shine the light of truth on the lies, manipulation, doubt, fear, and oppression that the Devil is sending against you. What is the truth in the situation you are facing? Not what are all the things that could go wrong in your situation. But what are the actual true elements in your situation. So many times I find people who are overcome by imagined fears, possible outcomes, supposed connections, potential facts that possibly cast doubts. This is the Devil's specialty. Don't fall for it. I like to remember when I am facing these forms of attack, the definition of F.E.A.R.: Fanaticized Exaggerations Appearing Real. Don't get worked up about what is not real. Reality (truth) is essential to keeping your wits about you. Truth cuts through the fog of lies that the Devil is pushing into your life. As he sends lies and deception your direction, he seeks to build whole sections of your life on a lie to manipulate you. We have all watched people who have lived parts of their life as if a myth or superstition were true. The truth cuts through these fabrications.

Truth is one of the pieces of the Armor of God that every Christian should wear at all times. We have to always be ready to ask, "Is what this person is saying the truth?" "Is what I am thinking the truth?" "Is what I am worrying about really possible?" God has given you truth to cut through the lies and to keep you from being manipulated by Satan's schemes. Can't you imagine Paul being attacked and oppressed by wicked spirits trying to discourage him (2 Corinthians 12:7)? He overcame the attack when he focused on the truths that he knew: truths about God (2 Timothy 1:12); truths about himself (Romans 8:1; 3:23); truths about others (2 Timothy 2:10); and truths about the world around him (1 John 2:15-18). Being infused with the truth, you have an antidote to the lies, deception, and seduction of the enemy. When the Devil presses in to get you to think or do things that are not consistent with God or are not consistent with righteousness in general, you can focus on the truths of God (reject the lies) to overcome the pressure.

Look at these biblical examples of how the heroes of the faith used truth to battle the Devil to a stalemate that ultimately pushed him away. In this first reference, it is Peter's statement of the truth about Jesus that brings the blessing. God put this truth in Peter's mind and then Peter had the courage to speak it out.

> *He said to them, "But who do you say that I am?" Simon Peter answered, "You are the Christ, the Son of the Living God." And Jesus said to him, "Blessed are you Simon Barjona, because flesh and blood did not reveal this to you, but My Father who is in heaven. I also say to you that you are Peter and upon this rock I will build My church; and the gates of Hades will not overpower it."* Matthew 16:15-18

Jesus tells us that the truth about what the Devil is doing and has done will be revealed eventually. The truth is that God has redeemed our souls, giving us the ability to resist compromising.

> *If they have called the head of the house Beelzebul, how much more will they malign the members of his household! Therefore do not fear them, for there is*

> *nothing concealed that will not be revealed, or hidden that will not be known.* What I tell you in the darkness, speak in the light, and what you hear whispered in your ear, proclaim upon the housetops. *Do not fear those who kill the body but are unable to kill the soul; but rather fear Him who is able to destroy both body and soul in hell.* Matthew 10:25-28

Jesus was accused of working for the Devil when He cast out demons. He answers them with logic and truth. He doesn't say a bunch of theological statements; He just reasons with them from what is obvious about things they have clearly not thought through.

> *But when the Pharisees heard this, they said, "This man casts out demons only by Beelzebul the ruler of the demons!" And knowing their thoughts Jesus said to them, "Any kingdom divided against itself is laid waste; and any city or house divided against itself will not stand. If Satan casts out Satan, he is divided against himself; how then will his kingdom stand? If I by Beelzebul cast out demons, by whom do your sons cast them out? For this reason they will be your judges. But if I cast out demons by the spirit of God, then the kingdom of God has come upon you. Or how can anyone enter the strong man's house and carry off his property, unless he first binds the strong man? And then he will plunder his house."*
> Matthew 12:24-29

In this verse Jesus addresses the Pharisees about an accusation they made against Him. Jesus was saying that they had given into the Devil's promptings; so much so, that they became his agents! Jesus states the truth about what they were saying—it was all lies. Notice that He does not yell or have an elaborate ceremony. He just states the truth.

> *You are of your Father the devil and you want to do the desires of your father. He was a murderer from the beginning, and does not stand in the truth because there is no truth in him. <u>Whenever he speaks a lie, he speaks from his own nature. For he is a liar and the father of lies.</u>* John 8:44

One of the most important bedrocks of Christianity is Jesus' statement about truth. It is spoken in connection with defeating the myths, superstitions, and lies that people have believed that keep them in bondage to the Devil. Truth cuts through nonsense.

> *So Jesus was saying to those Jews who had believed Him, "If you continue in My word, then you are truly disciples of Mine; and <u>you will know the truth and the truth will make you free.</u>"* John 8:31,32

If you are going to cut through the Devil's deception and manipulation in your life, you are going to have to embrace truth at a new level. Jesus said that you shall know the truth and the truth shall set you free. **Are you ready to embrace truth?** Are you ready to learn the truths about your life so that you can move forward into the blessed life that God has for you? Truth is a spiritual weapon that will cut away at the things that have been holding you back.

When a demonically-inspired magician in Acts 13 opposes the Apostle Paul, Paul waits until God the Holy Spirit gives him truth; and then he speaks that truth out, winning the day. Many of us hear God prompt us with the truth in various situations, but we are afraid to speak it out. Truth cuts through the bluster of the Devil's people.

> *But Elymas the magician (for so his name is translated) was opposing them, seeking to turn the proconsul away from the faith. But Saul, who was also known as Paul, filled with the Holy Spirit, fixed his gaze on him, and said, <u>"You who are full of all deceit and fraud, you son of the devil, you enemy of all righteousness, will you not cease to make crooked the straight ways of the Lord?"</u> (Then the Judgment of Righteousness was pronounced upon him.) "Now behold the hand of the Lord is upon you and you will be blind and not see the sun for a time."* Acts 13:8-11

The Apostle John tells us how to use truth to make sure that we are not being deceived. Find out what spirit is authoring the phenomena. Just because something is spiritual does not mean it is from God. Test the spirits. Ask the spirits real questions. I have found this test very helpful in cutting right to the heart of spiritual gifts and experiences.

> *<u>Beloved do not believe every spirit, but test the spirit to see whether they are from God...</u> and every spirit that does not confess that Jesus Christ has come in the flesh is not from God. This is clearly a truth test...* 1 John 4:1-4

I have watched many individuals break free from demonic oppression by injecting new levels of truth into their minds. Dr. Neil Anderson, in his excellent books and study materials that are a part of Freedom in Christ ministries, highlights the power of biblical truth. Dr. Andersen emphasized to me on a number of occasions the truth in 2 Timothy 2:24-26:

> *The Lord's bond-servant must not be quarrelsome, but be kind to all able to teach, patient when wronged, with gentleness correcting those who are in opposition, if perhaps God may grant them repentance leading to the knowledge of the truth, and that they may come to their senses and escape from the snare of the devil, having been held captive by him to do his will.*

It is all about truth. People need to encounter the truth of the Scriptures about God, about themselves, about the other people in the world, and it will set them free.

Spiritual Workout

Many times the truth you need is about who God really is so that you can escape the distortions that our world and your own mind develop about God. It is always helpful to be reminded from Scripture who God is. For further understanding of the truth about God, I have written a book called *Delighting in God* which will help you and there are other powerful books on this subject: *Knowledge of the Holy* by A.W. Tozer; *Knowing God* by J.I. Packer; *The Existence and Attributes of God* by Stephen Charnock. Let me give you a small glimpse of the power of truth about God. Look with me at Exodus 34:6,7:

> <u>Then the LORD passed by in front of him and proclaimed</u>, "The LORD, the LORD God, <u>compassionate</u> and <u>gracious</u>, <u>slow to anger</u>, and <u>abounding in lovingkindness and truth</u>; who keeps lovingkindness for thousands, who <u>forgives iniquity, transgression and sin</u>; yet He will by no means leave the guilty unpunished, visiting the iniquity of fathers on the children and on the grandchildren to the third and fourth generations."

Sometimes using truth as a spiritual weapon means reciting the truths about who you are in Christ. I am repeating an exercise from book two in the Weapons of Righteousness series, ***Ten Foundational Doctrines***, because it is so powerful. I remember one woman who was plagued by voices and nightmares. I assigned her to work through who she was as a Christian. She read over and over these truths. She looked up Scripture and she memorized these truths until she really embraced God's understanding of her in Christ and these truths set her free from the accusations, self-doubts, fear, and lies of the Devil. We have truly become a new creature in Christ. Who we were is covered in the new person that God is creating in Christ. The phrases are biblically true and should be read slowly over and over again. I cannot emphasize enough how the truth of who we are in Christ will thwart the Devil's schemes. Spend time looking up and reading the verses in the Bible where these truths come from.

Spiritual Workout

The Christian's Position in Christ

I am God's child. John 1:12
Having believed in Jesus as God, He accepts me as His child.

I am Christ's friend. John 15:15
He calls me His friend because He has revealed His plans to me.

I have been justified. Romans 5:1
I have been declared righteous through my faith in Christ's death.

I am united with the Lord, and I am one spirit with Him. 1 Corinthians 6:17
I have been bonded to Christ in a spiritual union, which is indissoluble.

I have been bought with a price. 1 Corinthians 6:20
I have been purchased at very great cost to God, so God sees me as valuable.

I belong to God. 1 Corinthians 6:19,20
God claims ownership over me so that He can set me free to live abundantly.

I am a member of Christ's body. 1 Corinthians 12:27
God has incorporated me into the mystical body of Christ presently operative on earth.

I am a saint. Ephesians 1:1
Because of my trust in Christ, God sees me as holy and set apart.

I have been adopted as God's child. Ephesians 1:5
I have been brought into the place of full privilege in God's family.

I have direct access to God through the Holy Spirit. Ephesians 2:18
I know that my prayers get through because of the Holy Spirit.

I have been redeemed and forgiven of all my sins. Colossians 1:14
I have been bought out of the slave market of sin and released from the ultimate penalty of my sins.

I am complete in Christ. Colossians 2:10
I have all I need because I need Christ. Together we are a perfectly sufficient unit.

I am free forever from condemnation. Romans 8:1,2
God does not condemn me because of my embrace of Christ.

I am assured that all things work together for good. Romans 8:28
God is powerful and brings good out of all the circumstances and even evil that barges into my life.

I am free from any charges against me. Romans 8:31
God will not listen to the Devil's charges against me.

I cannot be separated from the love of God. Romans 8:35
Nothing can separate me from the love of God that is Christ Jesus...NOTHING.

I have been established, anointed, and sealed by God. 2 Corinthians 1:21,22
God has planted me firmly to grow in Him. He has specially blessed me and marked me for heaven.

I am hidden with Christ in God. Colossians 3:3
My real life is hidden with Christ, and all I really am in Christ will be fully displayed when Christ returns.

I am confident the good work that God has begun in me will be perfected. Philippians 1:6
God has begun a process to make me like Christ and will not stop.

I am a citizen of heaven. Philippians 3:20
My true home is in heaven with Christ. I am out of place down here.

I was not given a spirit of fear but of power, love, and a sound mind. 2 Timothy 1:7
God has given me His Spirit to strengthen and empower me.

I can find grace and mercy in time of need. Hebrews 4:16
Every time I need God's power, His favor, His forgiveness, and encouragement, it is mine in Christ through prayer.

I am born of God, and the Evil One cannot touch me. 1 John 5:18
God gave birth to a new creature when I trusted Christ, and the Devil cannot touch that new creation.

I am the salt and light of the earth. Matthew 5:13,14
God has called me to help preserve what is right and good as well as to show the glory of Christ and how life should really be lived.

Spiritual Weapon of Truth

**I am a branch of the true vine, a channel of his life.
John 15:1,5**
God has connected me to His inexhaustible storehouse of energy, creativity, and power. All I have to do is stay plugged in to God, and all I need for any assignment will be available to me.

**I have been chosen and appointed to bear fruit.
John 15:16**
God chose me to be one of His children. I did not get in by mistake. He wants me to show the fruit of the Spirit in my life.

I am a personal witness of Christ's. Acts 1:8
God has empowered me to tell others what Christ has done for me.

I am God's temple. 1 Corinthians 6:19
God has established His eternal presence in my body.

**I am a minister of reconciliation for God.
2 Corinthians 5:17**
I have been asked by God to tell others that He is not holding their sins against them because Christ died for all their sins. They must accept Christ's payment.

**I am God's co-worker. 1 Corinthians 3:9;
2 Corinthians 6:1**
God has been willing to work with me to accomplish His will. He has in some sense restricted a part of His will to my cooperation. I am working with God.

I am seated with Christ in the heavenly realm. Ephesians 2:6
Christ says that I carry the same authority that He has as the one seated at the right hand of the Father. Every other being is under that authority, including the Devil.

I am God's workmanship. Ephesians 2:10
God is working on me to bring me to completion until He is completely satisfied and ready to enjoy eternity with me in heaven.

I may approach God with freedom and confidence. Ephesians 3:12
My ability to approach God is not dependent on my perfection but on Christ's finished work on the cross. I have freedom and confidence in Christ to come to God.

I can do all things through Christ who strengthens me. Philippians 4:13
There is not a job that God will ever give me where He has not also supplied all the power I need to complete that job.

Some have typed these truths out and laminated them so that they can say them over and over again. Others have taken this list and put it into their phone so that they can keep reading it over.

Sometimes using truth as a spiritual weapon means that everyone you know is a strange mixture of the image of God (Genesis 1:26) and sin and selfishness (Romans 3:10-13). People are capable of real good and awful evil. When the Devil influences a friend of yours to manipulate you or seduce you, it

Spiritual Weapon of Truth

is important that you are aware of this truth in order to combat the manipulation the Devil is running against you.

Let's apply this through an exercise. If you are angry or shocked at someone for something they did, ask yourself the question: Did they do this because they were trying to mess up your life (which is the definition of evil), or did they do this because they were being selfish (just wanting something for themselves)? Jesus dismisses and forgives those who crucified Him because He realized that they were just being selfish (trying to keep their jobs, following orders, trying to maintain their positions or way of life). Jesus said it this way while hanging on the cross, "Father forgive them for they know not what they do." I have had a number of people memorize this verse and say it over and over again while they watch people do selfish things. This helps you realize that other people are not looking out for you; they are looking out for themselves.

Sometimes using truth as a spiritual weapon means realizing that the institutions, authorities, advertisements, and amusements are not trying to help you but are trying to deceive you as to what is really important so they can gain an advantage over you (1 John 2:15-18). The applause, rewards, and encouragement of the world often move you in directions that are not righteous – not God's will – and are a colossal waste of time. Your friends will encourage you to have a relationship with a really beautiful but unrighteous person. The career advice you receive tells you to maximize your money or power but not your righteous impact or what you are really good at. All the advertising tells you that unless you are popular or famous, you are insignificant; so you want to sacrifice what you know is right to get more popular or more famous. Inject the truth of God into this lethal manipulation. *But seek first His kingdom and His righteousness, and all these things will be added to you.* Matthew 6:33

Spiritual Workout

What is the world and/or the Devil trying to get you to elevate way above its real importance?

Sports team, job, sex, designer clothes, popularity, grades, movie, relationship, money, power, looks, hobby, friends, marriage, children, membership to some group or club, being liked, some enjoyable activity, food, alcohol, good feelings, etc.

These things have importance in our life, but the problem comes when we try and make them too important and people and things that are truly more important are pushed down the level of importance to spend more time, money, and energy on these less important things or people.

Spiritual Workout

What truth do you need to learn, embrace, or re-embrace? You may only have a general idea of truth(s) you need to go deeper in the direction of... but keep going down that path as it will set you free.

Truth about God

Truth about yourself

Truth about others

Truth about the world

Key Truths

If you are going to use the first piece of the Armor of God - Truth - then you must fully embrace Scriptural truth. Truth is foundational to living free from the Devil's control. I will show you three key truths from the Scripture that must be incorporated into your thinking. You may want to read these verses over and over five times until you can repeat them without looking. Answer the questions about these key truths and let the truth of how your own choices have sown the seeds of your life. We are not puppets controlled by others. Yes, people can do unjust things to us; but we can still take responsibility for our life after the injustice has been done. What they did was unfair, maybe even evil, and seeking justice can be a part of making new choices. But we cannot sit down and just play the victim.

All kinds of people have been treated unjustly and yet have gone on to have highly successful lives full of love and compassion of others. In fact, there is not a tragedy or injustice you can name that we cannot point to someone who has had that very thing happen to them, and yet they overcame it through taking responsibility for their life from that point on. You did not cause the injustice, but you can control your reaction after the fact. Begin sowing good seed in your life and you will reap a harvest of an enjoyable life full of friends and loved ones.

If you wallow in misery and bitterness over what others have done, then the only seeds that will be planted will be by those who did you wrong and by yourself on the negative side. Take control of your choices and move forward. God has given you the power of choice and you are responsible.

Key Truth #1

You are responsible for every choice you made or didn't make

Galatians 6:7: *Whatever a man sows, this he will also reap.*

You choose the life you are living. You didn't choose all the components in your life, but you are choosing your life by how you respond to what is coming at you. Stop playing the victim. Stop blaming someone else. I have had a number of unjust and toxic things done to me during my life and career, but I found that only when I stopped blaming others for what I missed and began choosing how to build a great life from what I do have does the pain, the bitterness, and apathy stop. When I fully embrace the fact that I sow the field I stand in, I choose the life I live and I am set free to really live my life. God can and has empowered me to build a wonderful life out of the damage that others have done to it. Use the power of choice to move positively away from what has happened to you. You can choose differently and yet often it is just easier to blame someone else or something else. The truth is that the only thing you can control is you.

Spiritual Workout

What part of your life are you not taking responsibility about from this point forward?

Yes, you may be in a difficult situation because of others. Yes, you may be starting from a place that others don't have to start from. Yes, it may not seem fair because other people have more advantages. But you must take responsibility for your life and the choices you make as you go forward. Your choices are your responsibility from this point forward. You have the weapon of choice. Use it wisely.

You may be blaming someone for causing you to be in this place. You may be criticizing others for keeping you where you are. You may just have gotten used to whining about your situation and not doing anything to change it. Take full responsibility for your life from this point forward. Plant good seeds in your life and watch over time a crop of joy, love, and righteousness grow up and give you a great life.

Most of us are only a few righteous choices away from a significantly better life. Start taking responsibility for every choice you make. Also take responsibility for the choices that you don't take. If your boss passes you over for a promotion but you never ask why, then you caused the fact that you are not promoted the next time. If your spouse disrespects you physically, verbally, emotionally, or sexually and you don't say something or do something, then it will continue to happen and you will have chosen it. Use the power of wise choice to get the change that is needed.

The life that you are living is the direct result of choices that you made or didn't make three years ago. In fact, most of us can trace the choices that we made or ignored and how it caused us to be where we are today. If you don't like where you are today, then start making new choices so that three years from now you can be much closer to God's ideal for you.

In every situation and relationship you can do some different things to change your situation. You can say different things to change your situation. You can have a different attitude that will change your situation. Take responsibility for what happens in your life from this point forward. This one truth is so crucial to enjoying life and moving forward.

I know that it is so easy to just give in to the blame game or the victim mentality. But that will not build anything. It won't help you. When I have been faced with injustice, my natural reaction is to be angry and let others know of the injustice. But it is so much better to look for the choice that will move me forward. I may not have all the choices I want, but I always have at least one choice that will move me forward. Take it.

Key Truth #2

You have a purpose

Another one of the key truths that you and I must embrace in the deepest part of our soul is that we are here for a purpose. We have certain good works that we can do. Each of us was made to accomplish a purpose. When we do them, then all kinds of people benefit; and we benefit internally and externally. A soul that knows it is on its purpose is a satisfied soul. There is a dream inside each one of us about the impact that we can make. What is your purpose? What is your destiny? How are you supposed to make this a better world? What sphere or arena are you supposed to do the majority of your good works? This truth - that you are created for a purpose - is a spiritual sword, a spiritual laser that allows you to see and cut through the junk and get to the life you really want.

Many of us at times get sidetracked and distracted from our purpose, but there is always time to get back on track and back on purpose. Don't let the Devil tell you that you are too old, uneducated, married to the wrong person, or too far past your opportunity. It is not true. God has a way for you to get back on track, back pursuing your dream. There is a way and there are miracles that will appear to help you move toward your true purpose. It may be that you are supposed to help people medically; go after that. It may be that you are supposed to help people spiritually; go after that. It may be that you are supposed to make a difference by running a business. Your life is not just about eating, sleeping, and making money. You have a purpose. It may take you three to five years to get to the place where you can maximize your involvement. Start heading in that direction; you will be happier and more fulfilled as you head toward your purpose.

It is clear in a number of Scriptures that God has a purpose for each of us. We have a destiny that we can fulfill if we make the right choices. We have been designed to accomplish a number of positive things in this world. Just as fish were made to swim, saws were made to cut, and birds were made to fly, so we were made to do and accomplish specific things. We feel the pleasure of God when we are doing it. We sense meaning and purpose when we live it out. Our righteous destiny will produce positive and righteous outcomes for others as well as ourselves. Look at Ephesians 2:10: *For we are His workmanship, created in Christ Jesus for good works, which God prepared beforehand so that we would walk in them.*

The Devil, on the other hand, wants us to believe that we are accidents of nature and that we have no destiny, no divine good that we can accomplish, and that there are no significant things that we can do. This is a lie but the Devil gets lots of people to believe that they are just driftwood in the river of life. This snare of the Devil has caught millions of people; and they waste their opportunities, they harm others, and they miss the sense of joy and purpose that could be theirs.

Spiritual Workout

What is your purpose in life?

Why did God make sure that you were born?

What arena do you want to make a difference?

What is the righteous dream that God put in your heart?

Our purpose revolves around using our spiritual gifts, our abilities, our passions, our dreams, and our wisdom. Look at all of these areas and see what God has given you to do.

What are your spiritual gifts?

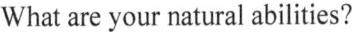

What are your natural abilities?

What are your passions?

What are your righteous dreams?

What are your experiences and wisdom?

Find your purpose and do it every day. Move toward your purpose every day. Your own soul will let you know when you are on purpose and when you are off purpose. It may be fuzzy at the beginning, but you will be able to increasingly say, "This is a part of what I am supposed to do!" I know that when I am involved in what I was made to do, there is an ease in doing it. Also time seems to go by quickly and other people tell me that I am good at it. When we have a dream and set goals to accomplish things in the direction of our true purpose, something just comes alive in us. Remember that your purpose may be completely different than those around you. It will always be righteous but it may be different. It could be medicine, law, sports, religion, education, counseling, business, politics, teaching, art, theater, engineering, music, design, landscaping, food, military, marriage, family, finances, planes, space…

There are a thousand things that God could have designed you to do that are good in the world, and you need you to do it. Don't just drift through this world, be on purpose and be about the right purpose. Be about the righteous purpose that God designed you for before the world ever began. Don't miss this. Life is not just about your having a good time. It is about your making a specific difference. Your life will take on a new joy and meaning when you are making that wonderful contribution you are supposed to make. You will be grasping and using the spiritual weapon of truth to defeat the Devil.

Key Truth #3

Life is Relationships

We are told that the one with the most toys wins. But that is not true. It is the one with the richest relationships that wins. Money and possessions are only valuable as they help us develop and maintain relationships. We have all watched countless movie stars or sports heroes who have money, prestige, possessions, and power but are miserable. People do not find stable enjoyable life until they find relationships of meaning and depth.

Building your career around your work instead of who you work with and who you work for will end in a very lonely existence. Embrace the truth of what Jesus tells us and use it as a sword of truth to block the Devil's lies. Life is relationships. The quality of your relationships is the quality of your life. It is true and it will always be true. If you are with people who don't want quality relationships, then your life can't move forward. If you are not pursuing quality relationships, then your life is not improving. Some people will not pursue a good relationship, and they may need to be removed from your life. This one truth will change your life if you fully embrace it and use it.

Jesus tells us that all of life is summed up in two commandments that are both about relationships. In fact, He specifically mentions increasing your love for three kinds of relationships in this condensation of all that God requires: Love God, love others, and righteously love self.

> Matthew 22:37: *And He said to him, "YOU SHALL LOVE THE LORD YOUR GOD WITH ALL YOUR HEART, AND WITH ALL YOUR SOUL, AND WITH ALL YOUR MIND. This is the great and foremost commandment. The second is like it, YOU SHALL LOVE YOUR NEIGHBOR AS YOURSELF."*

Jesus said it was one of the ultimate truths about the world and our lives: How are our relationships doing? We have ten major relationships. It is the quality of each one of these relationships that determine the joy and pleasure in our life.

Spiritual Workout

How would you rate the quality of your relationships on a scale of 1-10?

God (Spirituality)	1 — 2 - 3 — 4 — 5 — 6 — 7 — 8 — 9 - 10
Self (Body, Soul, Spirit)	1 — 2 - 3 — 4 — 5 — 6 — 7 — 8 — 9 - 10
Marriage (Romance/Affection)	1 — 2 - 3 — 4 — 5 — 6 — 7 — 8 — 9 - 10
Family (Immediate/Extended)	1 — 2 - 3 — 4 — 5 — 6 — 7 — 8 — 9 - 10
Work (Boss/ Colleagues)	1 — 2 - 3 — 4 — 5 — 6 — 7 — 8 — 9 - 10
Church (Leaders/ Friends)	1 — 2 - 3 — 4 — 5 — 6 — 7 — 8 — 9 - 10
Friends (Old/New)	1 — 2 - 3 — 4 — 5 — 6 — 7 — 8 — 9 - 10
Money (Income/Savings)	1 — 2 - 3 — 4 — 5 — 6 — 7 — 8 — 9 - 10
Society (Local/National)	1 — 2 - 3 — 4 — 5 — 6 — 7 — 8 — 9 - 10
Enemies (Past/Current)	1 — 2 - 3 — 4 — 5 — 6 — 7 — 8 — 9 - 10

We will never improve our relationships unless we aim at improving them. Just like the living room won't clean itself by hoping it will happen. You must do specific things to make a relationship grow, repair, and/or flourish. Yes, we can wait for the other person to go first, but that is not Jesus' advice. In the Golden Rule, "Do to others what you would have them do to you," Jesus tells us that we should go first with positive actions and see if we can push the relationship forward.

You do not want to get to the end of your life and then in heaven realize that it would have only taken a little apology to have a great relationship with your kids. You don't want to blow through multiple marriages and then afterward realize that if you had been kinder, gentle, and more understanding, you could have saved yourself a lot of heartache. It usually takes only a few small steps to move a relationship to the next level. Yes, the other person can reject our work but then it is them and not us. Romans 12:18 says *"so far as it depends on you, be at peace with all men."*

What are the relationships in your life that need to be given a little more time, energy, or resources? I know that you may want to give the time, energy, and money somewhere else but is God directing you to focus on a particular relationship?

As you look at the following list, focus on three changes - either positive or negative - that would make a difference in that relationship. One of the most interesting ways to get clarity about the three changes is to ask the other person what they think are three changes you could make to move the relationship forward.

Spiritual Workout

God: What three things could you do to improve this relationship? (Spirituality)

1.

2.

3.

Self: What three things could you do to improve this relationship? (Body, Soul, Spirit)

1.

2.

3.

Marriage: What three things could you do to improve this relationship? (Romance/Affection)

1.

2.

3.

Family: What three things could you do to improve this relationship? (Immediate/Extended)

1.

2.

3.

Work: What three things could you do to improve this relationship? (Boss/ Colleagues)

1.

2.

3.

Church: What three things could you do to improve this relationship? (Leaders/ Friends)

1.

2.

3.

Friends: What three things could you do to improve this relationship? (Old/New)

1.

2.

3.

Money: What three things could you do to improve this relationship? (Income/Savings)

1.

2.

3.

Society: What three things could you do to improve this relationship? (Local/National)

1.

2.

3.

Enemies: What three things could you do to improve this relationship? (Past/Current)

1.

2.

3.

Sometimes we have allowed relationships in our life that are so selfish and/or evil that we should not seek to repair them, but we should abandon them. They are corruptors of our life and do not help us move toward God but rather away from Him.

Spiritual Workout

Prayer for putting on Truth

Dear Heavenly Father,

I come to you in the Name of your Son the Lord Jesus Christ. I bow before You in complete surrender and ask that You would inject new levels of truth in my life so that I would be able to escape the snare of the Devil and cut through his manipulations and lies. I want to see my opportunities and choices with the clarity that You see them. I want to be set free by the truth from the prison of fear that keeps me from moving forward into the destiny that You have planned for me. I want the truth in my life, and I will adjust to it rather than cowering in the darkness not wanting to face reality about my life or my actions. It is only as I face the truth saturated in Your love that I will become the person You want me to be and live the abundant life You have destined for me.

There are things that are true about me that I do not know. There are things that are true about my life that I am unaware of. There are things that are true about my friends, family, and colleagues that I need to know if I am going to take powerful steps forward. These are not secrets, but I have just not been open to these truths before but now I am. I ask that You, Lord Jesus, powerfully arrange the truths that I need to know to come into my life, so I can embrace them and using Your power and love take my life to a new level.

I realize that I must embrace the truth that I am responsible for my life and for all of my choices. Please show me where I have blamed others for choices I have made or not made. Give me Your energy to make the righteous choices I need to make and have You guide me in the opportunities and decisions I need to make. I no longer want to blame others or play the victim. I realize that I did not cause everything that is a part of my life, but I am responsible for how I interact and react with everything. I can build a great life no matter the evil, injustice, or difficulty that has been thrown at me.

I want the truth to shine a light into my life and light the way that I should go. It is only then that I will be truly free. You have placed within me a purpose, a dream that was meant to guide me through my life. I am here on this earth for a reason. I am now ready to embrace that truth and harness it to pull me forward into the life You have for me. My purpose will be different than other people but it will benefit others. My purpose energizes and delights me. I no longer want to just get by in this world being distracted by the cares of this world. I aim to fulfill my purpose that You gave me. It is this truth that I am here for a purpose that will shine out of my life and give me the energy to push through the preparation and obstacles to fulfilling my purpose. I want You, Lord Jesus, to show me how to be on purpose and how to inject significance and meaning in my life through this truth. I know that my life will have a new resonance when I am on purpose just as the hammer does when it is hammering, the fish does when it is swimming, and the bird does when it is flying. This is what these things were made to do. I was also made to do something, and I am ready to embrace that truth. There are a number of good works that I was commissioned to accomplish, and I put on this truth and am empowered by it.

I ask You, Heavenly Father, to remind me and imbed in my soul the key truth that Life is Relationships. It is easy for me to get lost in the busyness and things of this world and lose sight of the preeminent truth that it is all about relationships. Your Son, the Lord Jesus, taught us that in the two great commandments that it is all about loving You, loving others, and righteously loving ourselves. I have lost sight of that at times, but I no longer

Spiritual Weapon of Truth

want to forget that truth. If I am building the right relationships in the right way, then I am making progress in my life. If I am gaining the whole world but destroying my relationship with You, others, or myself, then I am stupid. Shine this truth of relationships importance in me and out of me.

I come to You, Lord Jesus, and pick up the challenge to delight in God so that You will give me righteous desires and then fulfill those righteous desires. It is truth that we so often distort: "You really do want to bless us!" "You really do want to strongly support us!" "You really are for us!" "You want us to have an abundant life." I embrace this truth of Your desire to build into my life a testimony of Your love for me. I surrender to You and take delight in You so that your love and support of me will not be distorted by bad priorities on my part. I take up the truth that if I abide in You or delight in You or give You my whole heart, You will powerfully and strongly accomplish in my life what I could never accomplish and people will see You in my life. I want Your righteous blessing so that people can see You in my life. It is hard to imagine that my lack of goals and faith in You limits Your work in my life and Your reputation through me. I pick up the truth of trusting You for big things and righteous things so that people can see You repair, heal, develop, give, provide, teach, accomplish, and deliver. When I have in the past settled for what I could figure out and accomplish, I was submitting to the lies of the Devil. I no longer want to live under that cloud of deception. I want the truth of my great God's power and presence to lead me into things that are too big for me to accomplish but no problem for You.

In the Name and through the Blood of the Lord Jesus Christ, Amen

Chapter #3
Spiritual Weapon of Righteousness

Righteousness is another piece of the Armor of God that is to be worn at all times. Christians having and using righteousness as a spiritual weapon has two components. The first and primary element of righteousness comes from God through Jesus Christ's work. The second form of righteousness is our actions of righteousness. Righteous actions are a powerful spiritual weapon. They cut through the manipulations, sinfulness, and evil desires of the Devil. Any righteous actions on our part are powered by and based in the perfect righteousness of Jesus Christ. But if we are not righteous after Christ has done so much for us, then we will be attacked and we will be vulnerable.

It is absolutely essential that each of us understand that without Jesus Christ we are utterly unrighteous before a holy God (Romans 3:10-13). We cannot please Him and we cannot enter into His presence. God fixed this huge problem of our unrighteousness by having Jesus Christ live a perfect life and voluntarily give up that life, trading it for the sins of the world. Therefore the unrighteous can become righteous by embracing Christ as their way into the presence and good graces of God Almighty. Also, because of Christ those who abide in Him can do many righteous things. Even though Jesus the Christ is perfectly righteous and has qualified you for heaven through your faith in Him, if you do not begin to live out righteousness in your life, you will be vulnerable to satanic attack, temptation, and manipulation. The Devil will not want you to do righteous things that Christ prompts you to do. The Apostle Paul reminds himself that without Christ he is nothing and even one of the worst sinners (1 Timothy 1:12-15). But he realizes that he can do all things through Christ who is strengthening him (Philippians 4:13).

Let's take a look at how Jesus, the apostles, and other heroes of the faith used the spiritual weapon of righteousness to resist the schemes of the Devil. Notice in this first example that Jesus points out that Peter's self-focus is actually blocking righteousness. Peter is self-focused and wants the Lord to do what he wants instead of what is best for the whole world. Jesus needed to think of everyone, and not just a few, in order to love the whole world. The Devil used Peter to try and get Jesus to focus on a few people He dearly loved and ignore the much greater good He could do by dying for the whole world.

But He turned and said to Peter, "Get behind Me, Satan! You are a stumbling block to Me; for you are not setting your mind on God's interests, but man's."
Matthew 16:23

Later in Peter's life he reminds the early Christians that when they are battling the spiritual battles against the soul, they need to remain righteous. Righteous behavior is essential to this spiritual war.

Beloved, I urge you as aliens and strangers to abstain from fleshly lusts which wage war against the soul. Keep your behavior excellent among the Gentiles, so that in the thing in which they slander you as evildoers, they may because of your good deeds, as they observe them, glorify God in the day of visitation.
1 Peter 2:11,12

Spiritual Weapon of Righteousness

Just after the Devil prompts Judas to betray Jesus, Jesus pushes back against the Spirit of Evil in the upper room by an act of righteous love. Jesus' example of love was righteousness at its finest, and it pushed the Devil out of the room. Unfortunately because of his own choice to be greedy, the Devil did not leave Judas' heart.

> *During supper, the devil having already put into the heart of Judas Iscariot, the son of Simon, to betray Him, Jesus, knowing that the Father had given all things into His hands, and that He had come forth from God and was going back to God, got up from supper and laid aside His garments; <u>and taking a towel, He girded Himself.</u>* John 13:2

In the book of Acts when the Devil was working through a magician named Elymas on the island of Cyprus to block the message of the gospel, Paul pronounced a righteous judgment against him (that he would not see the light of the sun for a time).

> *But Elymas the magician (for so his name is translated) was opposing them, seeking to turn the proconsul away from the faith. But Saul, who was also known as Paul, filled with the Holy Spirit, fixed his gaze on him, and said, "<u>You who are full of all deceit and fraud, you son of the devil, you enemy of all righteousness,</u> will you not cease to make crooked the straight ways of the Lord? (Then the Judgment of Righteousness was pronounced upon him). Now behold the hand of the Lord is upon you and you will be blind and not see the sun for a time."* Acts 13:8-11

When a person embraces sin over and over again, they give it a place in their life. It is this lack of righteousness that provides the Devil a base of operations to begin working in their life. When this happens use the weapon of righteousness, confess your sins, and you will push the Devil from his place in your life.

> *Therefore, laying aside falsehood, speak truth each one of you with his neighbor, for we are members of one another. Be angry and yet do not sin, do not let the sun go down upon your anger, and <u>do not give the devil an opportunity</u>. He who steals must steal no longer but rather he must labor, performing with his own hands what is good, so that he will have something to share with one who has need.* Ephesians 4:25-28

Every elder will be pressured by the Devil to be conceited because of his position in the church. The new convert should not be subjected to that demonic temptation, so he shouldn't be put into such a position until he can learn that righteousness remains humble.

> *...and not a new convert, so <u>that he will not become conceited</u> and fall into the condemnation incurred by the devil.* 1 Timothy 3:6

Look at Job's life and the hedge of protection that God put around him. It was there because of the righteousness that Job lived out. This was not Job going to church; it was Job living a righteous, God-fearing life as a businessman. Righteousness was the weapon that helped build the hedge of protection.

> *There was a man in the land of Uz whose name was Job; and that man was <u>blameless, upright, fearing God and turning away from evil</u>. Seven sons and three daughters were born to him. His possessions also were 7,000 sheep, 3,000 camels, 500 yoke of oxen, 500*

female donkeys, and very many servants; and that man was the greatest of all the men of the east. His sons used to go and hold a feast in the house of each one on his day, and they would send and invite their three sisters to eat and drink with them. When the days of feasting had completed their cycle, Job would send and consecrate them, rising up early in the morning and offering burnt offerings according to the number of them all; for Job said, "Perhaps my sons have sinned and cursed God in their hearts." Thus Job did continually. Now there was a day when the sons of God came to present themselves before the LORD, and Satan also came among them. The LORD said to Satan, 'From where do you come?' Then Satan answered the LORD and said, 'From roaming about on the earth and walking around on it.' The LORD said to Satan, 'Have you considered My servant Job? <u>For there is no one like him on the earth, a blameless and upright man, fearing God and turning away from evil.</u>' Then Satan answered the LORD, 'Does Job fear God for nothing? <u>Have You not made a hedge about him and his house and all that he has, on every side</u>? You have blessed the work of his hands, and his possessions have increased in the land." Job 1:1-10

Spiritual Workout

Using Righteousness as a Spiritual Weapon

There are at least three ways to use righteousness as a spiritual weapon. The first way is to be covered in the ultimate righteousness of God. This type of righteousness only comes through faith, confessing that we need God to be our Savior (Romans 4). Becoming a Christian through embrace of Jesus Christ as one's personal Savior and Lord is a hugely powerful spiritual weapon. So let me ask you: Have you asked Jesus Christ to be your Savior and your Lord? If you don't know or you are not sure you did it right, why not do it now?

Dear Lord Jesus,

I admit to You that I am a sinner and have no hope of heaven without You. I ask You to be my Savior and Lord, forgive me of my sins, and make me the kind of person You want me to be. Thank You for dying on the cross for me.
Amen.

Spiritual Weapon of Righteousness

Spiritual Workout

The second way to use righteousness as a spiritual weapon is to make righteous choices and stay within the moral boundaries of righteousness. The moral boundaries of righteousness have been classically understood as the Ten Commandments. If you are regularly violating the standards of conduct given in the Ten Commandments, then you have made yourself vulnerable to demonic attack, demonic temptation, and/or demonic manipulation.

Ask yourself: Are there any aspects in my life where I am clearly living outside of the moral boundaries of the Ten Commandments?

- ☐ Do you worship other gods than God Almighty: Father, Son, and Holy Spirit?
- ☐ Do you bow down to images, statues, or representations of God?
- ☐ Do you deny you are a true follower of God by how you live or how you use His name?
- ☐ Do you gather at least weekly with other believers to worship God and physically rest?
- ☐ Do you give proper honor to God-given authorities in your life?
- ☐ Do you use violence or the threat of violence to get your way?
- ☐ Do you involve yourself in sexuality outside of a biblical marriage?
- ☐ Do you steal from other people or do you have stolen items in your possession?
- ☐ Do you lie or deceive others for personal gain?
- ☐ Do you scheme about how you can gain someone else's possessions?

If we allow these ethical violations to remain in our lives, then we allow the Devil openings to attack, tempt, and manipulate us. If you are presently guilty of any of these breaches, then figure out a plan how you will stop doing this.

The third way to use righteousness as a spiritual weapon is to practice "positive righteousness." Jesus Christ defines "positive righteousness" as loving God and others (Matthew 22:37,38). Are you loving God? Are you loving the people God has put in your life? Would the people say that you are actively loving them or that you are self-focused? Positive righteousness strikes a spiritual blow against selfishness and the work of evil. Love and its accompanying qualities change the environment and the relationships.

Spiritual Workout

Loving God has classically been defined as practicing the Spiritual Disciplines. Here is a list of many of these disciplines. If a person truly loves God, then they will practice more and more of these spiritual disciplines. Which ones are you regularly practicing? Which ones do you need to add to your spiritual formation plan? Each one of these allows the Christian to move into the presence of the Lord in different ways.

- [ ] Disciplines of Confession: Personal, Family, National
- [ ] Disciplines of the Holy Spirit: Guidance, Wisdom, Impossible, Anointing
- [ ] Disciplines of Interaction: Bible Study, Prayer
- [ ] Disciplines of Biblical Meditation
- [ ] Disciplines of Service
- [ ] Disciplines of Togetherness: Worship, Fellowship
- [ ] Disciplines of Identification: Communion, Baptism, Witnessing
- [ ] Disciplines of Abstinence: Fasting, Solitude, Sleep, and Silence
- [ ] Disciplines of Need: Love and Giving

Spiritual Workout

Loving others is best understood as pursuing, pleasing, and meeting the needs of another person. We don't often think of the fact that whenever we truly love another person, we have struck a powerful blow for God. We have also made ourselves more protected from spiritual attack. Look at the relationships in your life. Are you truly loving those people or just trying to extract what you want from them? Pray and think about each person in these relationship categories and whether you are loving these people. Put a checkmark by the ones you are truly loving and ask God to show you how you can inject more love into the ones that you are not currently loving.

- [ ] Self
- [ ] Marriage
- [ ] Family
- [ ] Work
- [ ] Church
- [ ] Friends
- [ ] Society
- [ ] Enemies

How are you doing with these three components of righteousness? Have you truly become a Christian by asking Jesus Christ to be your Savior and boss of your life? Are you living within moral boundaries of the Ten Commandments? Are you increasing the amount of love for God and love for others in your life?

Righteous Actions

What righteous behaviors do you need to do to live a righteously loving life?

As we saw in the section on the spiritual weapon of truth, God has marked out numerous good works for each of us to do (Ephesians 2:10). These mark out our purpose. Righteousness is a spiritual weapon that destroys evil, affliction, oppression, and injustice; but it must be individually applied by the people in a situation. It is not enough for Christ to be righteous. At some point the individual Christian must begin to act in righteous ways because Christ is empowering them. If we are truly Christian, then the righteousness of Christ empowers us to act in righteous ways; and we must cooperate with God in these ways or we are left open to the attack, manipulation, and oppression of the Devil even though Christ was totally righteous and died for us. The Christian judge must turn away from the bribe. The Christian husband must say no to the affair and love his wife. The Christian teen needs to turn away from pornography and let a safe adult help him develop a positive set of actions rather than get sucked into perverted love.

If we never act in righteous ways, then the spiritual weapon of righteousness does us no good because we have never picked it up. The Devil does not tremble when Christians talk about Jesus' righteousness or someday doing righteous things themselves. But he becomes fearful when Christians begin to act in righteous ways in the everyday of their life. The Devil wants us to talk about what Jesus did but not to do righteous things ourselves. If we never greet a stranger with kindness, we leave righteousness rusting in the corner. If we never give to the poor, we are unpracticed at righteousness when it is needed. If we do not give up time on our hobbies because our kids need time with us, then the righteous love that should have been injected into their heart never occurs.

Righteousness is not selling all you have and moving to Africa. Righteousness is the small sacrifices of love, the extra compliments, the words and time that are the right thing to do but so often go undone. Yes, it is also resisting the temptation to sex, gambling, corruption, anger, laziness, drugs, and arrogance. But righteousness always means putting a positive in the place of the negative. Don't think that you have finished acting righteously just because you have not sinned in some way. Do the positive that should fill that space or time.

Jesus goes out of His way to tell us that some of the most devastating critiques on judgment day will be for the sins of omission that we should have done but did not do. We were too selfishly absorbed to really love others (Matthew 25:31-45). Listen hard for the whisper of the Holy Spirit to help someone. Listen especially hard for his suggestion to love those closest to you. What righteous behaviors is God whispering that you should do?

Righteous Behaviors

You only have two basic options to increase righteousness in your life.

1. Eliminate unrighteous things from your life

2. Add more righteous loving actions to your life.

Spiritual Workout

One of the places that I regularly start with those who are under spiritual attack and want the protection of Christ and His righteousness is to get them to clean out their house or apartment of occultic things.

Step 2: CLEANING OUT YOUR HOUSE

The following is a suggested list of items that may be in your home which can give the Devil an advantage in your life. The scriptural method for destroying these objects is by smashing and/or burning (Exodus 32:19,20; Judges 6:25-28). This renders the objects unusable and therefore unwanted by another. It is recommended to pray after the objects have been destroyed and state the command: "Satan and the demons are no longer welcome here and must leave in the name of the Lord Jesus Christ. Whatever ground or place may have been given to Satan through my possession or use of this object is canceled and given completely over to the Lord Jesus Christ to be occupied by the Holy Spirit."

Occult Statues

There are a number of statues which are not idols in the classic sense but have strong occult ties and overtones. These would include the following statues:

wizards, trolls, demons, bats, serpents, witches, evil castles, ghosts and goblins, gremlins. All types of tapestries which glorify evil or satanic practices.

All these types of statues should be removed from the home of the Christians. It does not matter whether the statue is a cute version of a satanic creature; it should be destroyed and removed. One of the greatest deceptions is that cute things cannot be harmful. Remember, your home should be a place of safety and refuge, not a battle ground. Your home should be safe for the weakest Christian to find shelter and comfort.

Occult Objects

The secular marketplace is filled with objects that have occult significance. These objects induct the unwary into Satan's realm and have no business in the home of the Christian. It is a false hope to believe that a Bible on the shelf counteracts all occult objects.

Crystals (used for channeling power), Ouija boards, tarot cards, pyramids, pentagrams, good luck charms, amulets, egyptian worship symbols, talisman, astrology charts.

All these objects are used to call upon Satan and his demonic hordes, and they should not be treated lightly. Christians should not use, glamorize, or promote the occult in any way.

Occult Jewelry

There is an abundance of jewelry with devils, dragons, bats, skulls, and other strongly occultic themes which should be destroyed. There is no reason why a Christian should wear the marks of death and satanic bondage. Christians should proclaim in every area of life that they belong to the Lord Jesus Christ and have chosen to walk in the kingdom of light. There are certain types of jewelry which are not occult in their form but which have been made for or used in mystical or demonic religions (this would include some American Indian jewelry). This type of jewelry should not be owned, worn, and should be destroyed.

Occult Books

There are many different types of occult books from the New Age literature to the Satanic Bible which should be removed from the house. These books detail practices of evil. They can also act as place of operation for oppressive evil spirits. The list grows longer every month. If you believe a book, magazine, or article is satanic or evil, don't have it in your home. It doesn't matter that it is valuable. Get rid of it.

Pornography

This would include all types of pornography from soft core (airbrushed pictures of scantily-clad women) to hard core (graphic depictions of sexual relations). Pornography also includes written material which contains no pictures but describes sexuality or sexual acts in a seductive, alluring, immoral, or degenerate fashion.

Cult Books

There are many books produced which are not overtly occult or demonic but pervert the truth of God and the faith once delivered to the saints. Unless God has called you to a specific ministry of dealing with these groups, these books should not be in your home.

Music

There is a great debate about various types of music and its impact on Christians. Any music which arouses immoral, violent, or sinful desires is to be discarded. Any music which details satanic practices or offers praise to Satan or demons is to be discarded. Any music which captivates one's mind so that little room is left for meditation on the Scriptures and the Lord Jesus Christ is to be discarded. Each individual must examine every piece of music to which he/she listens.

Occult Practices

The most obvious area to receive demonic attachment or demonic oppression is involvement in the occult. Each area of involvement in the occult should be brought before the Lord in confession, repentance, and renunciation. Christians need to cut themselves off spiritually from these practices and enter into full adoption in the family of God.

Righteous Affirmations

Making positive and righteous affirmations of what we want our behaviors to be is incredibly powerful in building a great spiritual protection in our life. These righteous affirmations trigger the brain to move in these directions. It doesn't matter that when we start saying them, we are miles from actually living them out. We do need to want to be like these biblical affirmations. We are many times trying to do some huge righteousness when it is the little daily ones that add up and make the most difference.

I have found that the Fruit of the Spirit is a key list of righteous behavior that can always be added to our lives to increase the power of God and diminish the work of the Devil (Galatians 5:22,23). Listening to the prompting of the Holy Spirit to live out one of the fruit of the spirit is swinging a sword of righteousness for a brighter future. I have also found that the Beatitudes (listed in Matthew 5:3-12) are also a key definition of righteousness. These qualities of Christ-likeness destroy the Devil's work and bring spiritual protection. I personally will say these verses at least once a day. You may not notice anything right away, but your subconscious is seeing these affirmations as goal statements and it is moving you toward these qualities. Others will begin to see them appear in your life.

Spiritual Workout

On each of the following pages are basic Christian affirmations for each relationship in life. You will notice that they follow the major relationships of life: God, Self, Marriage, Family, Finances, Work, etc. Pick one relationship you need to make changes in and begin saying the affirmations at least once a day. Stay on that one relationship for a month. You will feel the pull to move your actions to match up with these affirmations. Good, let it happen. Keep making these affirmations and keep letting them be goals in the battle of righteousness. Every time you move in one of these directions even in the smallest ways you swing the sword of righteousness.

- Every day I have an intimate encounter with God because of the forgiveness in Jesus Christ where He guides me in my everyday life.

- Every day I present my life to God the Father, the Son, and the Holy Spirit and He directs me on how to improve it, enjoy it, and bless others.

- Every day I confess my sins through a classic guide or the Scripture I am studying that day.

- Every day I listen for the guidance of the Holy Spirit through the fruit of the Spirit, the wisdom literature (Psalms/Proverbs), or the Scripture God directs me towards.

- Every day I study a passage of Scripture and let God inform, encourage, and/or command me.

- Every day I meditate on a Scripture through slow repetition, study, personalization, confessionalize, singing, recording insights, diagramming, or writing my own translation.

- Every day I worship God through praise, adoration, thanksgiving, or exaltation.

- Every week I have fellowship with three types of believers: those who know more than me, those who know the same as me, those who know less than me.

- Every day I interact with God through prayer of all kinds.

- I look to serve God spontaneously every day, in my church every week, in my community every month.

- Every week I participate in corporate worship and/or communion and am ready to tell the testimony of my faith in the Lord Jesus.

- Every year I am open to God prompting me to fast, solitude, silence, or no sleep to pray for a matter of greater urgency and impact.

- Every week I am willing to rent my body to Jesus so that He can love people through me that I might not want to love.

- Every week or pay period I set aside tithes and offerings to honor God and develop a generous heart.

Fruit of the Spirit

I meet the needs of the key people in my life, pursue their soul, and please them (love)

I am looking for the positive and to deepen my relationships (joy)

I create harmony and calm (peace)

I give God time to give me wisdom and make key changes (patience)

I love and serve others with pleasantness (kindness)

I make sure that others benefit from my words, actions, and attitude (goodness)

I have impulse control and make thoughtful requests and wise adaptations when things don't go as I expected (meekness)

I trust God, looking for His direction and provision when the path is difficult (faithfulness)

I say no to my selfish desires and yes to righteous impulses (self-control)

The Beatitudes

I am grateful, teachable, and humble (poor in spirit)

I focus on my positive talents, gifts, and abilities realizing I also have significant areas of non-strength and need to team with others

I have processed my sins, wounds, and losses (mourn)

I am flexible, not demanding my own way

I have impulse control and make thoughtful requests and wise adaptations when things don't go as I expected (meekness)

I remain calm when others are emotional and reactive

I really want what it is right to happen, and I act to make it happen -- especially in key areas God alerts me to

I quickly forgive people's mistakes, wrongs, and attacks

My soul is full of positive, pure, and loving images

I think positive and pure thoughts (pure in Spirit)

I create harmony and calm everywhere I go

I am gladly willing to be insulted, wronged, and hated to stand up for what is right

I openly identify as a follower of Jesus Christ even if it brings insults and hatred.

I sacrifice to live within the Ten Commandments and resist abuse

If you are interested in progressing further in the Beatitudes, I would suggest that you look at my book, ***Deep Happiness,*** for a much fuller treatment on the Beatitudes.

Marriage

I have a delightful loving relationship with my wife because:

I honor her every day by complimenting her specifically about her, tell her I love her, and pass her priority test.

I live with her in an understanding way by apologizing when I have offended her, helping her accomplish her goals, and encouraging her to fully maximize who God made her to be.

I build her security in our relationship by making sure our finances are in the black and growing; never comparing her unfavorably with other women; resisting the temptation of flirting, pornography, and affairs; and never directing my anger at her.

I build incredible unity between her and I by always being on the same team with her (she cannot be the enemy), making sure she has far more positive experiences that we have done together than negative times, and asking her at least once a year where I might grow.

I have set up a system of decision-making that gives her confidence that a wise decision will be made if we initially disagree about something.

I nurture my wife and my marriage to maximum development by:

> Creating a one-hour appointment every day to actively listen to her
>
> Taking her on a date once a week to pursue her soul and have fun
>
> Tenderly touching her every day in many non-sexual ways

I defend and protect my wife and my marriage every day by:

    Praying God's protection with, for, and over her

    Teaming with her to block tempting influences in her life

    Helping remove toxic people from her life

    Teaming with her to eliminate draining circumstances and situations

For further treatment of these affirmations read my book ***Becoming a Godly Husband.***

I have a delightful and loving relationship with my husband because:

I respect my husband every day by mentioning his good points, accomplishments, strengths, and/or the temptations he has avoided.

I adapt to my husband by helping fill in the gaps where he is not perfect, knowing what he is good at and not expecting him to become something he can never be.

I help lead our home by my significant contribution to the domestic elements in our life.

I provide and even initiate sexual intimacy with my husband every two-five days, keeping his sexual focus on me.

I accompany my husband in activities, social occasions, and interests of his weekly and/or regularly.

I continually attract my husband to me and our marriage through the development of my soul and body by:

    Becoming more grateful, curious, and kind

Through colors, fashion, hair styles, nutrition, and exercise

I set aside time each week to be my husband's confidant -- the person to whom he can tell his side of the story, share his emotions at his speed, his dreams, and his disappointments.

For further treatment of these affirmations, read the book ***God's Radical Plan for Wives*** by Dr. Gil Stieglitz, Dr. Dana Stieglitz, and Jennifer Edwards.

Family

I have a wonderful, loving family because: I am an EP²IC parent.

Every day I ENGAGE with each of my children

Spiritually: Praying with and for at bedtimes each evening

Mentally: Teaching and helping them with homework

Emotionally: Listening to their stories, emotions, and desires

Physically: Playing with, practicing with, hugging

Vocationally: Assigning chores, working with, volunteering with

Financially: Giving allowances, playing monetary games, teaching

Relationally: Dating, knowing their friends, removing some friends

Every week I PROVIDE for my children

Spiritually: Praying with them each night and taking them to church

Mentally: Getting them into a good school and classroom, limiting TV time (two hours per evening)

Emotionally: Giving them someone wise they can open up to if not a parent

Physically: Time, equipment, and space to play informally and formally

Vocationally: Assign chores, explain my work, and get them skills and/or jobs

Financially: Give money for chores, teach income management, giving principles, and make sure that they tithe their money

Relationally: Finding good friends for them

Every week I PROTECT my children

Spiritually: Praying with them each night, taking them to church and having them recite the Ten Commandments

Mentally: Limiting their exposure to immoral or ungodly media

Emotionally: Listening to their feelings and showing them how to channel their feelings

Physically: Providing safe neighborhood, safe home, safe school, and safe friends…

Vocationally: Not allowing laziness, choosing the work environment, and getting their first job for them

Financially: Having them handle and budget real money and limiting spending

Relationally: Vetting teachers, spiritual leaders, and friends

Every week I INSTRUCT my children

Spiritually: Devotions at the dinner table nightly, bringing them to church, reciting the Ten Commandments, Lord's Prayer, Beatitudes, Fruit of the Spirit at the dinner table

Mentally: Stopping after each TV program and asking what it was selling? Interacting with their teachers to help the instruction process. Getting them tutors if they need them. Purchasing resources they need to grow and develop

Emotionally: Every emotion provides energy for some positive action; find it. Every emotion also provides energy that can be used destructively, so it must be limited and the energy put back in the positive channel

Physically: The dangers of traffic, strangers, molesters, criminals, authorities, etc., through role-playing, teaching, training, observations, programs, facts

Vocationally: Hard work, good bosses, bad bosses, teamwork, leaving well, etc.

Financially: Eight income streams, biblical wage range, types of income, avoid debt, make a budget, pay taxes, pay yourself, give tithes, give offerings, become generous

Relationally: Bad company corrupts good morals; hang around with successful people in the field you want to pursue. Be the person that attracts successful positive people

Every Week I CORRECT my children

Using the various methods to bring about a responsible choice the next time.

I realize that my correction will change as each child is different and each one changes as they grow up.

Post the following list on the refrigerator so that you are never far away from the possible training possibilities as the need may arise:

- Reset expectation
- Verbal repetition
- Practice
- Intense emotional reminder
- Isolation
- Time out

Spiritual Weapon of Righteousness

Chastisement

Rewards

Three-Battle Rule: after three battles, stop the war

Three-Day Rule: children can't keep pushing on something for three days if you are consistent with boundaries

Focus on one or two behaviors per week

Punishment fits the crime

Removal of privileges

Restraint: only used when they would harm themselves or others

Earned responsibility

The five questions:

1. What did you do?

2. Was it the right thing or the wrong thing?

3. What could you have done other than what you did?

4. What should be done so you remember to make a different choice next time?

5. What will you choose to do next time?

Work: Vacuuming the whole house, weeding in the yard, cleaning the grout on a counter top, dusting the whole house, etc. This gives them time to change their attitude.

Exercises: push-ups, sit-ups, jogging, step-ups, jumping jacks, etc.

No method of correction can be considered successful unless it causes the child to make a different choice the next time.

If you want further explanation on these acts of righteousness, please pick up my audio resources, **Becoming a Godly Parent** and/or **EP²IC Parenting**.

Finances

I am content, secure, and amazed at all the blessings God provides because:

I operate my finances in a biblical balanced manner following God principles for income management and generosity.

Every month I make sure that the following biblical income principles are at work:

    I stay within the biblical income range, usually seeking to maximize it

    I have 7+ income streams into my family

    I understand and operate my family as a business

    I refuse immoral, illegal, or unethical income streams

    Money is not the goal – relationships is the goal

    I pray for more income to accomplish righteous goals

Spiritual Weapon of Righteousness

Every month I make sure that the following biblical management principles are at work:

    I work to decrease my debt and/or stay out of debt

    I manage the money that comes to me through a reasonable budget

    I curb impulsive purchases by not allowing any purchase without 24 hours of prayer time

    I look for the best deal by comparing at least three brands or services

Every month I make sure that my family follows these biblical generosity principles:

    I know that God owns it all

    I tithe on my increase

    I give offerings to worthy causes

I would recommend ***Crown Financial Ministries***, ***Financial Peace Ministries,*** and ***YNAB.com*** as resources to understand these principles more fully.

Vocation / Work / Career

I enjoy a great career because I am following God's principles in my vocation.

I work hard every day being diligent – energetic – focused

I am a Team player – lowering ego – making the team win - playing the needed role.

I am Positive – about the company, about others, about bosses, about the product, etc.

I am Ethical – there are rules and boundaries that are bigger than profit or prestige

I am Relational – I learn and practice good people skills

I am Dedicated -- 110% -- committed -- willing -- sacrificial

I take time to make wise decisions where everyone wins (the wicked can lose)

Friends

I enjoy a rich variety of friends through using the seven friendship skills.

Every interaction I seek to find what I have in common with a person God has brought into my life

Every interaction with someone I am genuinely curious about the other person's interests, goals, and point of view and not just revealing my own

Every day I work hard to be positive, constructive, encouraging, and merciful. I do this by finding another way of saying criticism, condemnation, and/or complaint whenever possible

Every encounter I focus on the strengths of the person, minimizing their weaknesses

I am willing to educate my friend about a blind spot for their good

Every encounter with others I expect people to be selfish, and make mistakes. I am pleasantly surprised when they are not and forgiving when they are

I take the time before making a decision to look for wisdom -- the triple win. There must be a way that God wins, they win, and I win. Sometimes it takes a lot of looking

Spiritual Workout

Dear Heavenly Father,

I come in the Name of the Lord Jesus Christ asking that you would show me more clearly the righteous actions I can take that would push back the Devil's lies, manipulations, and temptations in my life. I want to swing the sword of true righteousness and drive the Devil away from decisions and opportunities. I realize that each time I act righteously in your power and your wisdom, I strike a spiritual blow. Show me the actions, words, and attitudes that I need to continue because they are making a difference in my life. Show me the actions, words, and attitudes that I need to do more of that can make a difference in the level of righteousness in my life and relationships. Open my eyes to see what I need to stop doing, saying, and giving off as an attitude that is damaging or destroying my relationships or my future. Cause me to understand and/or bring to me the actions, words, and attitudes I need to add to my life so that I will make new progress and new depth. All of these are the actions, words, and attitudes of righteousness that must become a greater and greater part of my life.

Lord Jesus, I want to be more sensitive to the places where I have missed out on righteous actions, words, or attitudes in the past. I realize that I need Your forgiveness for those and thank You for the forgiveness of Christ on the cross. I want to seize more of these opportunities for good. I will not be perfect like You, Lord Jesus, but I want to move forward in righteous behavior, growing more and more into Your image. Help me realize that every time I do, say, or give off a righteous attitude, I strike a blow for You, God. Even small acts of righteousness are not trivial; each use of the spiritual weapon of righteousness is a good thing. Show me more places to use righteousness as a spiritual weapon. Be in me and on me the spiritual power so I can truly be righteous in the ways it is needed in each relationship.

I know that righteousness is doing the right thing in each relationship. I ask You to give me the insight and energy to do the many little right things so that relationships and those people in my life can flourish. I want to swing the sword of righteousness so the Devil is kept at bay at that moment in that situation. Help me understand that the answer is to do the righteousness that is called for in that moment in that situation so the Devil will bleed to death from a thousand cuts.

In the Name and through the Blood of the Lord Jesus Christ, Amen

Chapter #4
Spiritual Weapon of Peace

God has chosen to make peace with us—to forgive us for our debt even though we could never repay it. This is the Gospel of Peace -- the third piece of the Armor of God that every Christian should wear at all times.

> *Now I make known to you, brethren, the gospel which I preached to you, which also you received, in which also you stand, by which also you are saved, if you hold fast the word which I preached to you, unless you believed in vain. For I delivered to you as of first importance what I also received,* **that Christ died for our sins according to the Scriptures, and that He was buried, and that He was raised on the third day according to the Scriptures,** *and that He appeared to Cephas, then to the twelve. After that He appeared to more than five hundred brethren at one time, most of whom remain until now, but some have fallen asleep.*
> 1 Corinthians 15:1-3

This Gospel of Peace should affect everything we do. God offers us forgiveness for all the ways we have and will offend Him. God was the one offended and yet He did the work for us. When we use the Gospel of Peace as a spiritual weapon, we can see it being used in two ways. The first way is to make sure that we are covered by God's offer of forgiveness. This means that we have embraced Jesus Christ as Savior and Lord accepting God's offer of peace with Him through the life, death, resurrection, and ascension of Jesus Christ. This is such a powerful spiritual weapon that the Devil will do all in his power to blind the minds of the unbelieving to keep them from seeing the wonder of peace with God through faith in the Lord Jesus Christ. This salvific use of the Gospel of Peace changes everything when a person embraces its power. Inviting Jesus Christ into our lives to create a relationship with God and justify us strikes a huge blow against the darkness.

There is a **secondary** use of the Gospel of Peace as a spiritual weapon that is also incredibly powerful. This is where a person makes peace with another person because they have been given the good news of peace with God. "How could I hold you guilty for your offenses against me when I have been forgiven so much by God?" We see this dynamic taking place in the following passage:

> Then Peter came and said to Him, "Lord, how often shall my brother sin against me and I forgive him? Up to seven times?" <u>Jesus said to him, "I do not say to you, up to seven times, but up to seventy times seven.</u> For this reason the kingdom of heaven may be compared to a king who wished to settle accounts with his slaves. When he had begun to settle them, one who owed him ten thousand talents was brought to him. But since he did not have the means to repay, his lord commanded him to be sold, along with his wife and children and all that he had, and repayment to be made. So the slave fell to the ground and prostrated himself before him, saying, 'Have patience with me and I will repay you everything.' And the lord of that slave felt compassion and released him and forgave him the debt. But that slave went out and found one of his fellow slaves who owed him a hundred denarii; and he seized him and

began to choke him, saying, 'Pay back what you owe.' So his fellow slave fell to the ground and began to plead with him, saying, 'Have patience with me and I will repay you.' But he was unwilling and went and threw him in prison until he should pay back what was owed. So when his fellow slaves saw what had happened, they were deeply grieved and came and reported to their lord all that had happened. Then summoning him, his lord said to him, 'You wicked slave, I forgave you all that debt because you pleaded with me. <u>Should you not also have had mercy on your fellow slave, in the same way that I had mercy on you?</u>' And his lord, moved with anger, handed him over to the <u>torturers</u> until he should repay all that was owed him. My heavenly Father will also do the same to you, if each of you does not forgive his brother from your heart." Matthew 18:21-35

This is a reasonable application of the Gospel of Peace coming to an individual. If you have received pardon from God for your offenses, you should then apply that pardon to the personal offenses in your life. This means that taking steps to make peace with others is a way to strike a spiritual blow for righteousness. It doesn't mean peace at any cost or peace which allows perpetrators to continue to abuse people, but it does mean that we are no longer holding personal offenses against people who have wronged us. There is an appropriate justice element so that perpetrators and other evil elements would be stopped. But notice that offering and making peace is a powerful spiritual weapon. It is important to realize that Jesus sees no difference between a person receiving the Gospel of Peace and the person using that Gospel of Peace to make peace with others.

Let me give you a few examples of what this looks like practically. When I became a Christian and admitted that I was a sinner with no hope of heaven without the Lord Jesus Christ and

His life and death for me, I used the spiritual weapon of the Gospel of Peace. If I help a person repent and embrace Jesus Christ as Lord and Savior, I have used the spiritual weapon of the Gospel of Peace. I also use the spiritual weapon of the Gospel of Peace if I forgive a person who has wronged me. I use the spiritual weapon of the Gospel of Peace if I help two people forgive each other or settle differences that were leaving them at odds. I have used the spiritual weapon of the Gospel of Peace when in the midst of the doubts and fear that the Devil throws at me, I remind myself that I have been forgiven by God and not because of anything I have done or not done but because of what the Lord Jesus Christ has done. When I delight in the fact of my forgiveness and acceptance by God through worship, praise, prayer, contemplation, and contrition, I am using the spiritual weapon of the Gospel of Peace. When I read the great passages of Christ's love for the world and His willing sacrifice for me, I am using the spiritual weapon of the Gospel of Peace. Read the verses below about Christ's sacrifice for us.

Who has believed our message? And to whom has the arm of the LORD been revealed? For He grew up before Him like a tender shoot, and like a root out of parched ground; He has no stately form or majesty that we should look upon Him, nor appearance that we should be attracted to Him. He was despised and forsaken of men, a man of sorrows and acquainted with grief; and like one from whom men hide their face He was despised, and we did not esteem Him. Surely our griefs He Himself bore, and <u>our sorrows He carried</u>; yet we ourselves esteemed Him stricken, Smitten of God, and afflicted. <u>But He was pierced through for our transgressions, He was crushed for our iniquities</u>; the chastening for our well-being fell upon Him, and by His scourging we are healed. <u>All of us like sheep have gone *astray, each of us has turned to his own way; but the LORD has caused the iniquity of us all to fall on Him. He was oppressed and He was afflicted, yet He did not open His mouth; like a lamb that is led to slaughter, and like a sheep that is silent before its shearers, so He did not open His mouth. By oppression and judgment He was taken away;* and as for His generation, who considered that He was cut off out of the land of the living for the transgression of my people, to whom the stroke was due? His grave was assigned with wicked men, yet He was with a rich man in His death, because He had done no violence, nor was there any deceit in His mouth. But the LORD was pleased to crush Him, putting Him to grief; if He would render Himself as a guilt offering, He will see His offspring, He will prolong His days, and the good pleasure of the LORD will prosper in His hand. As a result of the anguish of His soul, he will see it and be satisfied; by His knowledge the Righteous One, My Servant, will justify the many, as He will bear their iniquities. Therefore, I will allot Him a portion with the great, and He will divide the booty with the strong; because He poured out Himself to death, and was numbered with the transgressors; yet He Himself bore the sin of many, and interceded for the transgressors.* Isaiah 53:1-12

The next day he saw Jesus coming to him and said, "Behold, the Lamb of God who takes away the sin of the world!" John 1:29

For God so loved the world, that He gave His only begotten Son, that whoever believes in Him shall not perish, but have eternal life. For God did not send the Son into the world to judge the world, but that the world might be saved through Him. He who believes in Him is not judged; he who does not believe has been judged already, because he has not believed in the name of the only begotten Son of God. John 3:16

<u>*How blessed is he whose transgression is forgiven,*</u> *whose sin is covered! How blessed is the man to whom the LORD does not impute iniquity, and in whose spirit there is no deceit!* Psalm 32:1,2

<u>*Therefore, having been justified by faith,*</u> *we have peace with God through our Lord Jesus Christ, through whom also we have obtained our introduction by faith into this grace in which we stand; and we exult in hope of the glory of God. And not only this, but we also exult in our tribulations, knowing that tribulation brings about perseverance; and perseverance, proven character; and proven character, hope; and hope does not disappoint, because the love of God has been poured out within our hearts through the Holy Spirit who was given to us. For while we were still helpless, at the right time Christ died for the ungodly. For one will hardly die for a righteous man; though perhaps for the good man someone would dare even to die.* <u>*But God demonstrates His own love toward us, in that while we were yet sinners, Christ died for us.*</u> *Much more then, having now been justified by His blood, we shall be saved from the wrath of God through Him. For if while we were enemies we were reconciled to God through the death of His Son, much more, having been reconciled, we shall be saved by His life. And not only this, but we also exult in God through our Lord Jesus Christ, through whom we have now received the reconciliation.* Romans 5:1-11

Spiritual Weapon of Peace

> *<u>Therefore there is now no condemnation for those who are in Christ Jesus</u>. For the law of the Spirit of life in Christ Jesus has set you free from the law of sin and of death. For what the Law could not do, weak as it was through the flesh, God did: sending His own Son in the likeness of sinful flesh and as an offering for sin, He condemned sin in the flesh, so that the requirement of the Law might be fulfilled in us, who do not walk according to the flesh but according to the Spirit.*
> Romans 8:1-4

Our embrace of the peace with God that Jesus offers us should affect our bitterness, forgiveness, and peace with other people; or else we have not truly understood it and embraced it. It is not protecting us from the Devil's work unless it makes a real difference in our willingness to give peace to others who don't deserve it. Just as we were given peace when we didn't deserve it, so we must offer it to those who don't deserve it in our life.

Look at this extended passage on behaving as a Christian. So much of what it gives as advice for living in a sinful world filled with people who don't understand or like Christians is to be at peace with them.

> *Let love be without hypocrisy. Abhor what is evil; cling to what is good. Be devoted to one another in brotherly love; give preference to one another in honor; not lagging behind in diligence, fervent in spirit, serving the Lord; rejoicing in hope, persevering in tribulation, devoted to prayer, contributing to the needs of the saints, practicing hospitality. Bless those who persecute you; <u>bless and do not curse</u>. Rejoice with those who rejoice, and weep with those who weep. Be of the same*

mind toward one another; do not be haughty in mind, but associate with the lowly. Do not be wise in your own estimation. <u>Never pay back evil for evil to anyone</u>. Respect what is right in the sight of all men. <u>If possible, so far as it depends on you, be at peace with all men. Never take your own revenge</u>, beloved, but leave room for the wrath of God, for it is written, "VENGEANCE IS MINE, I WILL REPAY," says the Lord. "BUT IF YOUR ENEMY IS HUNGRY, FEED HIM, AND IF HE IS THIRSTY, GIVE HIM A DRINK; FOR IN SO DOING YOU WILL HEAP BURNING COALS ON HIS HEAD." Do not be overcome by evil, but overcome evil with good. Romans 12:9-21

Using the spiritual weapon of the Gospel of Peace means that you work hard at making peace with others. It means that you leave issues of justice to God and His God-given authorities. Do not be involved in the natural inclination to take your own revenge. The Devil really hates it when Christians begin to live at peace with God and others.

Let me say this another way: If I am a Christian and I enjoy the forgiveness of God but everywhere I go I create tension, strife, conflict, and even hatred, then I am open to demonic attack because I have not built the hedge of protection that is available to me through the forgiveness that is in Jesus Christ. If nothing about my life says "peace" or demonstrates that I am learning to make peace (Matthew 5:9), then I have a huge hole in my spiritual protection. I have seen God cover young Christians with His grace for a while as they learn to live out the forgiveness that He gave to them. But at some point He expects all of us to demonstrate forgiveness, peace, and harmony in our earthly relationships.

Spiritual Weapon of Peace

Jesus uses the spiritual weapon of the Gospel of Peace when the people want to stone the woman caught in adultery. "He who is without sin let him cast the first stone" (John 8:7). He may have been writing the names of their sins or the adulteress in the sand. In other words, if you say you have peace with God, it must affect how you treat your fellow man or you do not really have it.

Look at the Apostle Paul's insistence upon the ability to be gentle and peaceable with those who are under the sway of the Devil. The peace that emanates from the gospel fires a mighty weapon into their lives. It may dislodge the bondage they are under from Satan (2 Timothy 2:24-26). As God's bondservants we must be gentle, kind to everyone, and able to teach our opponents gently in the hope that God may grant them repentance and escape from the captivity that the Devil has them under to do his will.

Jesus also discusses the use of this spiritual weapon of the Gospel of Peace in the part of the Sermon on the Mount where He talks about vengeance and making peace with an enemy.

> *You have heard that it was said, "AN EYE FOR AN EYE, AND A TOOTH FOR A TOOTH." But I say to you, do not resist an evil person; but whoever slaps you on your right cheek, turn the other to him also. If anyone wants to sue you and take your shirt, let him have your coat also. Whoever forces you to go one mile, go with him two. Give to him who asks of you, and do not turn away from him who wants to borrow from you. You have heard that it was said, "<u>YOU SHALL LOVE YOUR NEIGHBOR</u> and hate your enemy." But I say to you, love your enemies and pray for those who persecute you, so that you may be sons of your Father who is in heaven; for He causes His sun to rise on the*

evil and the good, and sends rain on the righteous and the unrighteous. Matthew 5:38-45

Turn the other cheek... give him your cloak... go with him a second mile... do all you can to make peace with your enemy. You have been given so much...

Notice that Jesus suggests that a person go out of their way and even be wronged in order to bring about peace with someone they don't like or may even consider to be an enemy. This is using the spiritual weapon of the Gospel of Peace.

Another application of the spiritual weapon, the Gospel of Peace, is given to us by Jesus as He sends His apostles out on their first preaching and teaching ministry in Matthew 10:11-15. Notice that He tells them to look for the man who is worthy of their greeting of peace. This person has often been called the man of peace in that city.

> *And whatever city or village you enter, inquire who is worthy in it, and stay at his house until you leave that city. As you enter the house, give it your greeting. <u>If the house is worthy, give it your blessing of peace.</u> But if it is not worthy, take back your blessing of peace. Whoever does not receive you, nor heed your words, as you go out of that house or that city, shake the dust off your feet. Truly I say to you, it will be more tolerable for the land of Sodom and Gomorrah in the Day of Judgment than for that city.* Matthew 10:11-15

One of the questions that I regularly ask to try and activate this spiritual weapon of the Gospel of Peace in various counseling settings (marriage, personal, family, church) is:

What would it take for you to live in harmony and joy with this person?

I find it interesting that people often know exactly what it is that they must do to begin living in harmony with another person; but they refuse to do it because they don't want to give up some comfort, surrender that level of control, or they don't think the other person has earned that level of love. There are two general actions that are required to keep a relationship in harmony: I must limit myself in some way in order to stay in relationship with this person, or I must love them in some new way that I have ignored or have been resisting. Every relationship comes with benefits (my being loved), responsibilities (my loving the other person), and limitations (my refraining from certain things to stay connected to this person).

Sometimes a further question must be asked before one tries to make peace. Is there anything that requires immorality to be in harmony with this person? If I am required to violate God's moral laws, then I cannot be at peace with this person. But there is often a creative way of working toward harmony that does not involve violating God's law. Not in every case but in many. If the other person will not make peace with me unless I violate the law of God, then the spiritual weapon that needs to be fired is righteousness, not peace.

Spiritual Workout

There are other questions that can help you get a greater grasp of this incredibly powerful spiritual weapon:

- Is there a level of peace with God that you have neglected?

- Are you a Christian but you really haven't forgiven God for something that happened to you?

- Do you need to make peace with another person?

- Do you need to do something or stop doing something to harmonize with someone?

The Spiritual Weapon of Peace

What actions or strategies of peace / harmony do you need to do to live a righteous loving life?

The Devil is trying to keep us from God's loving plan for our lives by keeping us in disharmony, conflict, anger, and bitterness. If the enemy of our souls can keep us in constant turmoil about something, then we never make progress to what our life should be like. Do not let this travesty happen. Pick up the powerful spiritual weapon of peace and begin cutting away at the conflict, stupidity, and emotion that keeps you stuck in a dead-end place. Often we have not thought through or let God prompt us how we may be keeping peace from happening in our lives. We want to bring harmony and calm everywhere we go if it is at all possible.

Notice every time you take positive steps toward Christ and His future that some relationship will develop conflict in some way. This is how the Devil keeps you stuck. Peace is a weapon. The refusal to engage in the nonsense of the past can liberate you from relationships and circumstances that have been placed in your life by the enemy. Jesus Christ has paid for your peace with God. Use that peace to bring peace to your current relationships and circumstances. Gain peace with these people or move away from them if they won't move toward peace. Become a man or woman of peace.

There are only two choices which produce new levels of peace and harmony. I do not know which one you should focus on, but the key to new levels of peace and harmony lies in one of these. Don't wait for the other person to change. Make peace through your new actions or cessation of old actions.

1. Stop actions (actions, words, attitudes) **of disharmony**

2. Do actions (actions, words, attitudes) **of harmony**
Also realize that when you move in either one of these directions, you are swinging a powerful spiritual weapon. The Devil believes that you don't want harmony; He believes that you want your way at any cost. When you use the spiritual weapon of peace instead of the worldly weapons of anger, power, vengeance, and slander, God's power is revealed and something awesome happens.

Spiritual Workout

What disharmony should you stop?

1.

2.

3.

What harmony should you do?

1.

2.

3.

It is important that I talk about the situations where the one person wants hostility. There is often far more that we can do than we might think initially. But in the extreme cases where a person resists all attempts to make peace, then pursue peace by getting away from that person as much as possible. Don't jump to that strategy but it may be an option when the other ones we will discuss are exhausted.

Spiritual Weapon of Peace

Spiritual Workout

New peacemaking actions

1. Agree

There are times when you should agree with the other person even though you could disagree. The point is minor. It won't make a difference who is right. You took the other side just to play the Devil's advocate. Both positions are correct in some way. All you will accomplish in your disagreement is make the other person angry, look bad, or make you angry or you look good at the other person's expense. In so many cases the goal should be peace, not who is right.

Just say,

"You know, you are right."

"I am sorry for making a fuss about this."

"I have changed my mind and I agree with you."

"It is more important for me to be at peace with you than to pursue this anymore. You are right."

"I was wrong, you are right."

Practice saying these phrases so that you can use them when it is appropriate. If you do not say these phrases out loud a few times, you will not be able to say them when you need to… so go ahead and read them through three times.

2. Focus on where you agree 101%

There are some people and some relationships where you will never come to complete or even majority agreement. But you are in a relationship with them. Instead of focusing on the things that you disagree with this person about, focus on the things about which you agree. If you disagree about politics but agree about some social cause, then put 100% of your effort into talking about the social cause. If you disagree about a cultural issue or practice but agree on tax relief, then put your energy into talking about tax relief. It will always be tempting to bring up things that you think are right that you know they will not agree with but what is the point. If you already have had this discussion before and they will not change their mind and you will not change your mind, don't bring up those topics. If you agree on the kids but disagree about almost everything else, then focus on the kids. If you both like sports and can keep it civil when talking about sports, then put your connections there.

There are some friendships that will be only about work or only about a sports team or only about a particular cause. It is okay to have one-item friendships. Too often we look for places where we disagree with a person and wonder why we don't have more friends.

Who are you having a lot of difficulty with right now? What one issue or topic do you agree on with this person? If you don't know what the one topic is, then start seeking it in conversation so that you can build the relationship around that one issue, idea, or topic. Usually when you start looking for the one topic that you agree on, you will find more than one where you have significant common ground. There is no point in spending time with someone arguing when you could spend it discussing, exploring, and/or encouraging one another on the one topic that you agree about.

What do you agree on?

Sports, weather, clothes, fishing, children, good news, etc.

3. Thoughtful requests

One of the things that many people never discover is that other people are often willing to do what you suggest if it is presented in a thoughtful way instead of in anger, crying, or being manipulative or deceitful. If we are going to grow in our ability to produce harmony and peace in our relationships, we must get past just blurting out what we want the first time we think about it. We need to reflect on what it is that will help us and help the other person or party. Often this will take writing out a number of different practice or trial proposals before you have adequately captured a request that is reasonable, respectful, and inclusive. It is important that you get used to the idea that you will need to practice thinking through what you ask the other people in your life.

The following is a step-by-step procedure to work through your desires from raw "I want what I want" to "I am wondering if we could do this because it seems that everyone would benefit from this…" This requires that you control your emotions and be patient with yourself and the other person. Your selfish desire will always push to the front and demand that the other person just submit, but that rarely produces peace. Work through this process a few times until you can work through this in your head. Give it the time it needs. Sometimes it needs days, sometimes it needs weeks, and sometimes it needs months before you arrive at a truly thoughtful request that allows for true harmony.

1. Here is what you want in the raw.

    I want this….

2. Here is a different way to say that.

> I think it would be great if we did...

3. Here is a way that incorporates reasons why the other person might want it also.

> I know what you have been wanting to do... So I thought if we did... it would help in that direction.

4. Here are adjustments to what you want that will make it more acceptable to the other person.

> I believe that our family needs... and we could do this... and that would lead us to doing this other thing we also wanted to begin doing for the kids.

5. Here is how you will present a thoroughly researched and prepared request so that all parties win.

> I have looked at these articles and they say... we could do this if we were to do this other activity over here.

This process is called seeking after wisdom in the Scriptures.

4. Adapt

One of the many ways that the Devil blocks us from enjoying the loving plan that God has for us is by getting us stuck in old habits, old prejudices, old opinions of others, or an unwillingness to embrace the reality of a situation. The Devil wants us to go on protesting in various ways how people act, how they think, what they did, and never actually make decisions that could change these situations. We either need to adapt to these people and situations or make decisions to move away from these people and situations. Let's look at the example of Christ from Philippians 2:3-10. Jesus Christ is God and He decided to lay aside the use of His divinity and come to earth as a man. Think of how limiting that must have been for Him. Whatever He was used to as God, He no longer had those freedoms and opportunities. He had to adapt to His being a man. He had to adapt to all kinds of people who really didn't get who He was or why He was there. The Scriptures then go on to tell us that He wasn't just a man but a servant. He had to adapt to a different place in the authority structure. Yet He adapted to this demeaning level of authority. There were all kinds of situations and people who should have adapted to Him, but He had to adapt to them. He created peace wherever He went. Yes, He called out evil behavior on a number of occasions, and He did not ever refuse to adapt to situations for His own comfort or pleasure. Let's examine this crucial strategy that Christ gives us to create peace in our world.

Many times we do not have peace in our life because we refuse to adapt to the people and situations that are actually in our life. We so much want the people to be different or the circumstances to be better, so we just will not adapt to the reality of the people and circumstances. Ask yourself what it would look like if you just adapted to the people and/or situation you are in. There is nothing wrong with wanting things to be different, but often we have to accept where we are before we can move to someplace different.

List all the regular people in your life

Are there ways that you could adapt to them in some way

Talk to them differently

Act differently towards them or around them

Prepare for times with them in different ways

Do something different

5. Confront / Clarify

Another way that the Devil keeps us stuck far from God's plan for our lives is by getting us to over-adapt to people and situations. There are some behaviors, situations, and words that should be confronted. There are some people who so regularly bully other people that this abuse becomes the standard practice around this person. Making peace with another person should not involve adapting to abuse. To get to real peace you may have to confront abuse in its various forms. Some will not back off of their selfishness until they know that there are consequences to what they are doing. There are a number of forms of abuse that need to be confronted: physical abuse, verbal abuse, emotional abuse, sexual abuse, power abuse, property abuse. When you are in relationship with a person who does these things, then there can be no real peace until this is confronted and abandoned. Not everyone wants to play by ethical rules. They may like winning at others' expense, and they do not want to stop the abuse. If this is the case, then you will have to make the decision on how, when, and where you may exit from that relationship so you can find true peace in your life. I have seen people really help the abuser by taking a strong stand to not be involved with them until they deal with their behaviors.

What I am suggesting is that real abuse not be allowed to continue in your life. You may need help in working through confronting people in your life. If you are experiencing repeated and strong abuse, please see a counselor, pastor, or knowledgeable friend before you begin any confrontation. You will not find peace in your life in many situations until you are willing to step up and say that you felt demeaned, disrespected, or even abused by a particular behavior or particular words.

Spiritual Workout

Finding positive peaceful people

The Scriptures clearly declare in 1 Corinthians 15:33: *Bad company corrupts good morals.* Who we choose to hang around with often makes a huge difference in the level of peace in our life.

Make a list of the people you spend time with regularly: friends, relatives, family, colleagues, bosses, neighbors, church people, etc. Write down the names of these people individually. (*The Success Principles* by Jack Canfield, 10th anniversary edition, William Morrow Publishing 2005, 2015, page 230)

Put a (plus) by those people who give you energy or are a generally pleasant experience in your day.

Put a (minus) by those people who are cynical, negative, or critical.

Negative, cynical, and/or critical people leak a toxic flow into our life so that peace is not really possible. It may not be possible to eliminate all of the negative people from your life but limiting your exposure can make a huge difference when it comes to peace. Negative people do not want peace. They want something to complain about. They want problems to whine and be cynical about. Choose to get away from negative cynical people and be around positive peaceful people.

How are you going to eliminate or diminish the time with people who are toxic?

Simply by choosing to spend time around more positive people. You can change the spiritual temperature of your life. Simply limiting or eliminating the negative, cynical people can keep the Devil from having a way into your life.

Spiritual Workout

Bringing closure

Another tool for achieving peace using the peace of Christ is to bring closure to your unfinished events and relationships. Most of us have incompletes in our lives that we have never finished or properly closed. These could be relationships, projects, issues, events, and other things that were left in your past unresolved. I remember making a list of people I needed to apologize to and explain what happened. It was great to be free from those incompletes.

A majority of your incompletes will be people who were at one time in your life and for some reason that relationship needs closure in some way. I have had some people go back and pay for candy they stole from a store. I have had people apologize to their children for the times they were not there for them or were drunk in front of them. Some of these people may be deceased, but we have ignored closing that relationship. You may need to go to their grave and have a conversation and say the things that need to be said. This may involve asking for forgiveness and or confronting them with the truth.

You may need to call some people on the phone and apologize for how you acted in the past. You may need to let them know that it was not okay what they did in the past. You may need to close down a relationship that you just slipped away from and never really told the person you were moving on.

You may have to make amends for things you did or didn't do in the past so that it is no longer weighing on you. Some may even have to visit law enforcement and deal with issues and crimes from the past.

Make sure that your bringing closure to your issues does not endanger other people and their lives. You should just deal with your stuff. You do not have other people's permission to deal with their stuff (unless you do). You know what you did and what you didn't do and whether you need to finish up an issue from the past.

This may take a considerable amount of time, so give yourself the months or years to make the phone calls, to have the conversations, to make amends, to go back and deal with the situation. Peace is a powerful weapon and without peace, life can be a miserable grind. Many people who don't have peace try and overwhelm their lack of peace with pleasure and addiction. This is not a lasting cure but a destructive escape route for abandoning peace.

Spiritual Weapon of Peace

Spiritual Workout

Prayer to utilize the Spiritual Weapon of Peace

Dear Heavenly Father,

I come to you in the Name of your Son the Lord Jesus Christ. I want harmony and peace in my life. I want it with You, so I surrender my rebellious will to live my life Your way. There is no point in fighting You. I want to be at peace with You. I have been pushing back against what I think You want to do in this one area. I am ready to do it Your way. Teach me, lead me, and I will follow.

I know, Lord Jesus, that the Devil is right now trying to keep me from Your plan by getting me stuck in anger, strife, conflict, and bitterness with the people in my life. I choose to pick up Your peace and begin cutting away at the foolish and pointless issues that keep me from the kind of life You want for me. The Devil has stopped me too long through disharmony, anger, selfishness, bitterness, and conflict. Fill me with your peace and show me how to use this powerful weapon to glorify You in and through my life.

Lord Jesus, please show me the ways that I can achieve new levels of peace in the various relationships of my life. Do I need to stop something that I am currently doing? Do I need to do some new things that I haven't done or have not consistently done? I do not want to be at war with the people in my life. I am sure that I am unaware of a number of things that I am currently doing that are keeping one or more of my relationships in a state of agitation or even open hostility. Show me what I am doing so I can stop. Show me how I can adjust my behavior in wisdom so that the other people can adjust their behavior and we can have peace.

I ask You, Lord Jesus, to empower me to be like You and adapt to the people and circumstances around me and achieve a supernatural level of peace. I need Your energy and grace or I will fall back into doing things my way. You, Lord Jesus, were able to adapt to all kinds of people and circumstances that were clearly below You, and I want to have Your power to do that. Please walk with me and shut my mouth when I would say the wrong thing. Prompt me to do some new thing that would create peace. Open my eyes to see when I have adapted to wickedness so I can wisely confront it.

In the Name and through the blood of the Lord Jesus Christ, Amen

Chapter #5
The Spiritual Weapon of Faith

Faith is the first spiritual weapon of the second list of God's pieces of Armor. This is one of the weapons that does not need to be used constantly, but it should be ready to be picked up for use at a moment's notice to deflect an attack from the Devil or to move forward against significant spiritual opposition. Notice the apostle's language in Ephesians 6:16:

> ...in addition to all, taking up the shield of faith with which you will be able to extinguish all the flaming arrows of the evil one.

This is a spiritual weapon to be used when spiritually you are under attack. It is so often called the shield of faith that many cannot think of it without the metaphor. But the spiritual weapon is faith. Too often the emphasis has been on the idea of a shield rather than faith. It is faith that will allow us to extinguish the flaming arrows of doubt, fear, anger, depression, worthlessness, lust, and hatred. Faith is about moving forward. Faith is about risking and trusting our captain. Even in the Roman army the shield was for the defense of an offensive attack. Faith is a weapon in our spiritual battle because it allows us to move forward in a protected way.

There are two possibilities for what the apostle means by this spiritual weapon called "faith." It can mean the objective doctrines called "the faith" that were once delivered to the saints by Jude. It can also be the subjective trust in God (many times in spite of contrary circumstances, e.g., Job). Since the objective doctrines of the Christian faith are covered under the piece of armor called truth, it is better to see this weapon as <u>*subjective trust in God*</u>. When Satan attacks, it is critical that one possess a strong trust in the basic goodness and faithfulness of God. God will ask us in the midst of our spiritual battles to do things that will require us to trust Him. We will have to risk (trust) in order to defeat a particular temptation or overcome a particular fear.

When you face the temptation to give into porn or an affair, God may ask you to risk looking foolish by not indulging your sensual appetites. He may ask you to run away from the situation or the people. He may ask you to tell your spouse or someone else what is really going on. He may ask you to risk being alone for a long season rather than be with the wrong person.

When you face fear that wants to put you in a small, little life, God may ask you to express your faith by going right into the face of the fear and doing the fearful thing. He may want you to trust Him that a few safe people need to know what you are going through. He may want you to risk looking stupid by removing yourself from a situation or relationship that consistently produces fear.

The message of Scripture must be believed even in the face of difficult, if not impossible, circumstances. God will whisper the risks that He wants you to take. They are all based on Scripture, but they mean that you must trust God rather than the messages around you or your own desires many times. Being a Christian takes faith, it involves risks, and it means that you trust God when it is easier to go the world's way. Realize that defeating the Devil involves Christian risks. You must use the spiritual weapon of faith, or you won't make it out of your own spiritual front yard. Life with God means trust, risk, and faith. It is faith that protects and cuts through the prison bars of fear, doubt, ease, and comfort.

The Spiritual Weapon of Faith

I have had the privilege of working with a wonderful organization, Courage Worldwide, which rescues girls who have been forced into sexual slavery. As these girls are rescued from the streets, they are put into a group home where they are cared for and taught that life doesn't have to be the way they have been experiencing it. There comes a point where they have to risk everything about "how life works" and decide that they want to learn a new way of life. If they don't have faith or trust, then they will return to their former way of life even though they know it will destroy them in the next few years.

As a pastor I work with all kinds of people who are at crossroads in their life. They need to make new choices, find new friends, move to a new place, believe that they are smart enough to go back to school, say no to an old flame, change the way they dress, and a million other options. If they are unwilling to take the risk and express their faith and trust God for their future, they fall back to their old patterns and get the same results that they have been getting. They usually blame God for why their life is not better, but they decided to not trust Him. They decided to not go after the new life they could have had.

What is God asking you to trust Him for?

Simple trust in God is necessary and must be developed in order to sustain the Christian life. When Polycarp, the early church father who was personally discipled by the Apostle John, was captured and threatened with death if he did not renounce Christ, he replied, "Eighty and six years have I served Him and He never did me any injury. How then can I blaspheme my King and my Savior?"[1] The spiritual weapon of faith is available to new believers, deepening as time is spent walking with God.

---

[1] Tan, P. L., *Encyclopedia of 7700 Illustrations: Signs of the Times* (Garland: Bible Communications, Inc., 1996), 787.

Answers to prayer, diligent study of Scripture, and careful observation of nature and circumstances all help to strengthen faith. The book of Job describes a man who utilized all these methods to develop an unshakable faith in God.

We must show believers how to develop and express faith rather than just talk about the need for it. Too often churches spend time explaining faith but do not demonstrate how to develop faith or how to express it in the midst of satanic attack. Like Peter walking on the water, Christians under attack must learn to keep their eyes focused on the Lord Jesus and take the risk Jesus is asking them to take. We must come to trust God in the midst of the working out of His plans for us. We don't always see the evidence of how it will all work out before we must trust Him.

Faith is the ability to "hang on until morning." In the book of Lamentations, Jeremiah says in the midst of the darkest circumstances: *For His compassions never fail, they are new every morning. Great is Your faithfulness* (Lamentations 3:22b-23). It is the ability to believe God in spite of contrary circumstances which protects us from the devouring plans of the Enemy. It will take many risks to accomplish the will of God for your life. When Satan attacks, a simple and unshakable trust in Christ is essential.

I can picture the Apostle Paul remembering the times when he was under enormous pressure to deny Christ or cut and run from the physical persecution he was facing. I can see him trusting Christ. He knew what Christ had told him. He knew what the Scriptures said. Even though his personal situation was not pleasant or prosperous, he knew that he could trust God to work it all out. He had entrusted his soul to the one who could keep it and transmit it to heaven (2 Timothy 1:12). He had seen Christ come through for him time and time again; and just when it looked bleak, God came through with an earthquake, a miracle, a friend, or a message. He was so glad he had not given into the pressure of the demon.

Let's take a look at how Jesus and various heroes of the faith used this spiritual weapon to push back the Devil's attacks, temptations, and manipulations.

The Apostle Paul was using this spiritual weapon of faith when he penned Philippians 3:8: *...I count all things to be loss <u>in view of the surpassing value of knowing Christ Jesus my Lord</u> for whom I have suffered the loss of all things...*

He knew in the midst of the things that were difficult that God was the winner ultimately and he could trust Him. Look at 2 Timothy 1:12 and its clear use of this spiritual weapon: *For this reason I also suffer these things, but I am not ashamed; for I know whom I have believed and <u>I am convinced that He is able to guard what I have entrusted to Him until that day.</u>*

Look at the warfare taking place in the Garden of Gethsemane and how the Lord Jesus used the spiritual weapon of faith to ward off the oppression of the Devil.

> *Then Jesus came with them to a place called Gethsemane, and said to His disciples, "Sit here while I go over there and pray." And He took with Him Peter and the two sons of Zebedee, and began to be grieved and distressed. Then He said to them, "<u>My soul is deeply grieved, to the point of death; remain here and keep watch with Me.</u>" And He went a little beyond them, and fell on His face and prayed, saying, "<u>My Father, if it is possible, let this cup pass from Me; yet not as I will, but as You will.</u>" And He came to the disciples and found them sleeping, and said to Peter, "So, you men could not keep watch with Me for one hour? Keep watching and praying that you may not enter into*

temptation; the spirit is willing, but the flesh is weak." He went away again a second time and prayed, saying, "<u>My Father, if this cannot pass away unless I drink it, Your will be done."</u> Again He came and found them sleeping, for their eyes were heavy. And He left them again, and went away and prayed a third time, saying the same thing once more. Then He came to the disciples and said to them, "Are you still sleeping and resting? Behold, the hour is at hand and the Son of Man is being betrayed into the hands of sinners. Get up, let us be going; behold, the one who betrays Me is at hand!" Matthew 26:36-45

The writer of the book of Hebrews tells us how Jesus used faith while crucified. Jesus took a risk that if He surrendered His life, then it would open the way for all those who would believe in Him to have access to the Father. Look at Hebrews 12:1-3:

Therefore, since we have so great a cloud of witnesses surrounding us, let us also lay aside every encumbrance and the sin which so easily entangles us, and let us run with endurance the race that is set before us, <u>fixing our eyes on Jesus, the author and perfecter of faith</u>, who for the joy set before Him endured the cross, despising the shame, and has sat down at the right hand of the throne of God. For consider Him who has endured such hostility by sinners against Himself, so that you will not grow weary and lose heart.

The Apostle Peter uses this spiritual weapon of faith as he and an increasingly small number of disciples continue to follow Jesus even after He has said a number of things that cause the multitudes and the fair-weather disciples to leave. The Devil looks to be winning as many turn away from Jesus, but Peter speaks for the core group.

The Spiritual Weapon of Faith

> *As a result of this many of His disciples withdrew and were not walking with Him anymore. So Jesus said to the twelve, "You do not want to go away also, do you?" Simon Peter answered Him, "<u>Lord, to whom shall we go? You have words of eternal life. We have believed and have come to know that You are the Holy One of God.</u>"* John 6:66-69

I find it powerful that Peter doesn't pretend to know what Jesus meant by the things He said. He had no answer for what Jesus was doing; all he knew was that Jesus was the Holy One of God and he was following in faith. The Devil could twist what Jesus said and the Devil could force many of the disciples to choose their own logic and their own understanding of the spiritual world to disqualify Jesus as the Messiah, but this would not affect Peter. He had faith and was using it.

Job uses this spiritual weapon of faith as he faces the Devil's onslaughts. Notice how he clings to his understanding and trust in God:

> *Be silent before me so that I may speak; then let come on me what may. Why should I take my flesh in my teeth and put my life in my hands? <u>Though He slay me, I will hope in Him.</u> Nevertheless I will argue my ways before Him.* Job 13:13-15

Spiritual Workout

If you are under spiritual attack from temptation, fear, doubt, manipulation, depression then one of the ways out will surely be faith. This means: What risk and actions of trust is God wanting me to take so I can escape this pressure and start moving toward a righteous loving life?

1.
2.
3.

In order to be fully alive and enjoying God's best, you must be prepared to take risks that push you just past your comfort zone. If we only do what we are comfortable with, then we will live lives that are imprisoned by our emotions (fear, frustration, comfort). God wants to stretch us. He has a plan full of good works and love for others that requires that we become bigger people than we are right now.

God wants you to pursue some breakout goal in at least one area.

What one thing - if God and you were to accomplish it -- would change everything in your life for the positive?

The Spiritual Weapon of Faith

Spiritual Workout

Overcoming Reasons, Fear, and Obstacles

Every time any of us think about doing things beyond our comfort zone, immediately we think of a number of reasons why it won't work. These "reasons" are what has been stopping you from pursuing God's best. You will need to face these "reasons" if you are going to win in your battle with the Devil. What is interesting is that these "reasons" readily come to mind and you can write them down and examine the things that have been stopping you. There are usually three categories: reasons, fear or other emotions, and obstacles. It is the weapon of faith that will cut these opponents down.

Write down one of the risks you think God wants you to do and then write down all the objections to doing it that come to your mind. It could be something like going back to school. It could be looking for a serious relationship. It could be changing jobs. It could be to no longer put up with your spouse's drinking.

Risk:

Objections:

1.
2.
3.
4.
5.

6.

7.

8.

9.

10.

Look at this list. These are the things that have been stopping you from a new life. Some of them are connected to a past event in your life. Some are nonsense. Some sound logical but you have never really looked into whether it is really true. Some of them are emotion based. Some of them are real obstacles that would need to have a work around to move forward.

I have found that if we cry out to God about our desire to trust Him we can ask Him for ways to work with each of these objections. If this is really Him wanting you to move in this direction, then you are asking for His power and wisdom to deal with these objections. Any time God asks you to trust Him for something new, you will have to work through this kind of exercise.

The Spiritual Weapon of Faith

Spiritual Workout

Where is God asking you to take a risk – to step out in faith?

I have included some of the things God has often said to others in these relational categories. This is not all He might be saying, but you might prayerfully read through the list.

Spirituality

Set aside time for God, use your spiritual gift more, meditate on the Bible more, serve in some new capacity, increase one or more of the fruit of the Spirit, worship God in new ways, fellowship with other Christians differently, ask God for more, witness, communion, baptism, increase your generosity, confess your sins.

Your list:

Personal Development

Go back to school, go to a counselor, get a life coach. Get a degree, certification, new training of some kind. Develop a different body image, fashion change, different nutrition. Process the pain of past wounds, losses, and changes. Make crucial decisions you have been putting off. Increase your safety. No longer allow mental, physical, or sexual abuse. Choose to righteously love yourself.

Your list

The Spiritual Weapon of Faith

Marriage / Romance

Acknowledge the value of your spouse. Treat your spouse as of supreme value. Accept your spouse for who they are without wanting them to be someone else. Understand your spouse in ways you have not. Adapt to the reality of living with your spouse. Include your spouse's perspective in your thinking and planning. Gently lead and guide your spouse's soul. Create a peaceful home. Understand and work with your spouse's sexual needs. Listen with attentiveness to your spouse's interests. Protect your spouse from people, situations, and issues that are overwhelming for them. Work hard to make decisions that are mutual. Provide all that your spouse needs to grow and fully develop as a person.

Your list:

Family

Engage with the members of your family spiritually, mentally, emotionally, physically, and relationally. Provide for your family in new ways spiritually, mentally, emotionally, physically, and relationally. Protect your family in new ways or at new levels spiritually, mentally, emotionally, physically, and relationally. Instruct your family so they can be a successful family spiritually, mentally, emotionally, physically, and relationally. Correct your family about things that they are doing, or are about to do that will not result in good for them or others.

Your list:

Vocational

Work harder. Relate more to key people. Develop new levels of people skills, change positions, change employers, start your own business, take training, learn new skills, be more agreeable to your supervisors, go above and beyond what you are called to do, go back to school, do what you have always wanted to do.

Your list:

Finances

Increase your income, develop more than one income stream, look at new opportunities. Increase your management of your money, budget in a new way, stop spending on things that don't last, look for less expensive options. Get out of debt. Become more generous, give a tithe of your income to a church or charity, look for a charitable cause you can invest in.

Your list:

The Spiritual Weapon of Faith

Church

Lead at church more or in new ways. Evangelize in new ways. Help people connect with the church. Lead a home group or teach a class. Serve in a new way. Give more or help others give. Worship God at new levels at church. Love others inside and outside the church Make sure that the church is on Jesus' purpose and not just playing church.

Your List:

Community

Be involved in my community or nation in recovery, prevention or justice at new levels than previously, striving to be salt and/or light to those around me.

Your list:

Friends/Enemies

Loving those who are my enemies. Increasing the breadth and depth of my friends. Eliminating some friends who are destructive to a righteous life.

Your list:

Real Christian joy and love always involves risks. It will always be a little tension producing to follow Christ. The great stuff in life is usually on the next rung of the ladder. Take the risk. Defeat the Devil's small vision for your life.

Chapter #6
Spiritual Weapon of Salvation

All of us have been offered a way of escape from the wrath of God for our rebellion and sins. This is called salvation. The salvation that is offered in the Lord Jesus Christ is the crucial spiritual force that gives us access to all other spiritual weapons. Christ's ultimate salvation is not ways of escape that God offers in this life. All of us have experienced God's financial, vocational, relational, and even emotional blessings. We were stuck in some way and God offered a way out. The most obvious example of the other forms of "salvation" that Christ offers is found in 1 Corinthians 10:13 when the apostle says:

> *No temptation has overtaken you but such as is common to man; and God is faithful, who will not allow you to be tempted beyond what you are able, but with the temptation <u>will provide the way of escape also</u>, so that you will be able to endure it.*

The word translated "way of escape" in 1 Corinthians 10:13 is the Greek word *sozo*, which is the word "salvation" or "deliverance." What we understand by this verse is that if God allows us to be tested or tempted, He always provides a practical way out of that difficulty so we do not have to sin. Therefore there are two aspects to this spiritual weapon called salvation: Jesus is the ultimate way of escape and specific way of escape for particular situations. It is both of these salvation aspects that we want to explore under the title "salvation."

When God tells us of the spiritual weapon of salvation, we need to understand that it is not just a mental weapon to help us as we are on our way to heaven. Satan is scheming against us in every part of our life. We need all forms of Christ's *salvation* in all the parts of our life. We need the wonder of God's gift of forgiveness and righteousness to penetrate into every aspect of our life. We also need lots of specific ways of escape as we live our life with God: relational ways of escape; financial ways of escape; ways of escaping temptation; societal ways of escape; ways of escaping our own weaknesses and lack of judgment. Christians need to start looking for these ways of escape and taking them so that they can foil the Devil's plans.

The spiritual weapon of salvation is another type of weapon (like faith) which does not need to be worn at all times but needs to be ready for "the evil day." There are some days that are more evil than others. For whatever reason on a particular day you are the target of a major spiritual attack or temptation. It is these days that you will need all God's ways of escape. This evil day may be about your ultimate salvation, or it may be about a more physical, emotional, or financial testing or temptation.

Let's spend some time discussing this spiritual weapon of salvation. In its ultimate sense, salvation is everything. Without Christ's death for our sins and offer of righteousness, we could have no contact with God. We would be cut off from the Almighty, and the Devil would win in every conflict. But because of Jesus' life and death, we can be spiritually reborn and enjoy an impossible life of love, mercy, wisdom, and joy. The internal war over our own salvation will eventually swing to the questions of assurance, present fellowship, and future hope. The Devil does not want us to be at ease over what Christ has done for us. It is so helpful for the Christian to understand their salvation in all of its aspects. Theologians tell us that there are at least twenty-seven separate concepts and/or benefits that come with the wonder of Christ's salvation (i.e., adoption, union with Christ, regeneration, election, resurrection power, etc.). Learning to take full advantage of these concepts greatly strengthens us in our spiritual war with the Devil. The Devil will attack the concept of God, the possibility of salvation, whether the individual is worthy of saving, and the assurance of salvation.

It is at this point that the Christian needs to understand the nature of justification. Salvation is not dependent upon the works or righteousness of the individual but upon the finished work of Christ on the cross. It is at this point that the doctrine of eternal security provides a great advantage in our warfare with Satan. As Spurgeon said, "At times I have such great bouts with depression that I assume that I am not saved, but my salvation does not depend upon me but on Christ's work on the cross." (Charles Spurgeon, *Lectures to My Students*). Knowing the details of our salvation in Christ keeps us from falling into the mental traps of Satan.

In order to utilize salvation as a spiritual weapon, the Christian also needs to understand the present outworking of salvation called *sanctification*. God is present and active in the life of the Christian, and they should cooperate with Him. Spiritual warfare often brings a sudden awareness of the Holy Spirit's promptings and conviction. One woman, who was raised in church, came to a deliverance session I was conducting at the insistence of one of our prayer team members. After the session she was shocked and stunned at the movement of the Holy Spirit during the meeting. During our prayer for the afflicted person she had a clear sense of how God was prompting her and how she fit into the prayers of the whole team. She was quite insightful and clearly guided by God and left with an entirely new understanding of the present ministry of the Holy Spirit. She told me that she had been taught to ignore those promptings of the Holy Spirit. As she began to discern the promptings of the

Holy Spirit, it revolutionized her life. In fact, the next day her Spirit-led prayers became instrumental in setting another believer free. The present ministry of the Holy Spirit is essential to living the victorious Christian life.

Another aspect of the present ministry of the Lord Jesus and the Holy Spirit in the life of the believer is the practical ways of escape that God orchestrates to escape the schemes of the Devil. I find that many Christians do not look for these ways of escape as they should. These practical deliverances are just as much a part of the spiritual weapon of salvation as receiving the forgiveness of God and escaping the wrath of God.

Let's take a brief overview of practical ways of escape provided in the Scriptures so that you can better identify God's provision of them for you. Cry out to God that He would provide them and that you would have eyes to see them. We see Noah being saved through the building of an ark. We see Moses being saved from arrest in Egypt. We see the two spies being saved in Rahab's house in Jericho. We see the young David being saved by God in a number of instances – like Abigail's quick action and good counsel and Saul's lack of detection and deep sleep. David was warned to leave the city of Keliah and he faked madness before King Abimelech. We see Elijah being saved from Jezebel by supernaturally outrunning her soldiers. Later birds help feed him, saving his life. We see Jesus being saved from His encounters with the Devil by angels that ministered to Him. We see Jesus being saved by passing through the crowds on numerous occasions when they meant Him harm or wanted to make Him king before the appropriate time. We see the Apostle Peter being saved from certain execution by an angel removing his chains and walking him through the corridors and gates until he was released in the streets. We see Paul being saved by being let down through a window in the wall surrounding Damascus. We see Paul later being saved by two hundred soldiers escorting him to Caesarea while under arrest. He was also saved through the gifts of the Philippian Christians. All of these and many other biblical salvations are the work of God for the believer to thwart the desire of the Devil. Believers have been witnessing God providing these kinds of salvations throughout history. The writer of Hebrews 11 states that physical salvation did not always happen and some were sawn in two; others were burned alive. God provides the ultimate salvation of escape from facing His wrath, but He also provides practical salvations; and we should cry out for them and expect them to be revealed to us.

A third aspect of the spiritual weapon of salvation is our future glorification in heaven. There is a future for the Christian. Jesus is coming back for His own people eventually. Regardless of what millennial or rapture position one holds, the Scripture says Jesus is coming back. Satan and his hordes are constantly trying to destroy a person's future both on this earth and in heaven one day. One of his tried- and-true strategies is to suggest that there is no reason to go on living and there is nothing significant to do, so a self-destructive activity should be pursued. They suggest that circumstances will not change, so why not commit a particular sin to redirect one's life? They promote a distorted and depressing picture of the future to defeat the Christian. All this can be resisted by a clear understanding of God's plan for abundant living here on earth and the future abode of the Christian. If we love the world too much and seek to make our fortune here, then we will be disappointed. In the midst of the most tremendous suffering and deepest personal pain when sin or suicide seems the only way out, a firm grip on our final abode will preserve us and defeat the designs of Satan.

Jesus and the apostles counted on God to provide salvation of all kinds in order to keep the Devil from winning...and so should we. Learn more about the amazing grace that God has given you in the Lord Jesus Christ. Begin to call upon and expect God to provide ways of escape so that the Devil does not win in your life.

Spiritual Workout

Jesus Christ the ultimate way of escape

Of all the help that God could send to this desperate world think about what He did not send. He did not send an army battling for righteousness physically. He did not send a physical weapon which made all believers in God invincible to their enemies. He did not send an angel to lock up the Devil in some way so that there would be no more temptations or spiritual oppression. And He did not send unlimited amounts of money to all believers in God. It is very instructive that God Almighty thought that the most important thing that He could do for us was to send us His Son and give us a way to connect with Him through faith. Therefore we must ask, "Have you fully embraced Jesus Christ as your only hope for escaping the wrath of God?"

If the answer to that question is no, then I would encourage you to pray a prayer seeking God to enlighten you as to your need for faith in the Lord Jesus Christ. And then when you have come to grips with your need to be reconciled to God, pray a prayer of faith asking God to forgive you of your sins and begin guiding your life as never before. Ask the Lord Jesus Christ to be your way of escape from the life and consequences of that life that you have been pursuing. Take a look at the various aspects of God's way of escape that are listed in the following pages. At some point in your spiritual journey you may be ready to pray a prayer like this.

Spiritual Weapon of Salvation

Dear Lord Jesus Christ,

I realize that I am a sinner and that I have no hope of heaven or reconciliation with God on my own. I need to be forgiven of my sins and You Jesus are my only hope. I ask You to be my Savior and bring me into right relationship with God. I am also asking You, Lord Jesus, to be the boss of my life. Guide my life and my decisions so that I can fulfill your loving plan for me. Come into my life and make me the kind of person you want me to be.

In the Name of the Lord Jesus Christ,

Amen.

Spiritual Workout

A deeper look at God's ultimate salvation in Jesus

Which aspect(s) of Salvation do you need to contemplate and practice in your life?

Read through the following aspects of your salvation through Jesus Christ. Learn how to take full advantage of salvation. These are designed to thwart the schemes of the Devil.

Exploring the full breadth of this spiritual weapon will revolutionize your life. The salvation of God is usually divided into three parts:

1) that which we have and are presently experiencing of God's amazing way of escape

2) that which is still future about our salvation and deliverance from our sins

3) that which God did before the world began and before we were born to prepare for His offer to us of our salvation

Read slowly through these brief descriptions and allow God to point you at the verses and aspects of His salvation for you that would be helpful for you to explore.

1. The Ministry of Conviction (reproof)

This is the work of God in the soul that suggests that all is not right in a person's relationship with God. This is the whispers of God into the soul of the individual that highlights a person's fractured relationship with God (Colossians 1:21; Romans 5:8), the reality of the spiritual world (Hebrews 11:6), their guilt before a Holy God (Romans 3:23). The goal of the whispers are to help a person see their need for a Savior to repair their relationship with God and set them on the right path in life (2 Corinthians 5:18,19; Ephesians 2:3).

2. God's Call

This is the whisper of God in the soul of the individual that there is a way back to God (Matthew 22:14), that now is the acceptable time to pursue God (2 Corinthians 6:2), that God accepts faith in Jesus Christ as Savior as a way to be reconciled to Him (Romans 5:8; Colossians 1:21).

3. Conversion

This is the miracle of God that when the work of God in preparation before the world began and the accomplishments of Jesus Christ as the God-man meet the sincere faith of the believer, the person becomes converted from what they were to a different person (Matthew 18:3). The person who was unacceptable to God is now acceptable. The person is seen by God in and through Jesus Christ and His righteousness (Romans 5:1,2).

4. Justification

At the same time that the person is converted from unacceptable in the eyes of God to acceptable in the eyes of God, God records this change as a declaration of the individual's righteousness (Romans 3:23).

5. Regeneration

This is another miracle of God where He injects into the soul and spirit of a person, new life that was not there before. This person is a new creation in the Lord Jesus Christ (Titus 3:5; John 3:16). The believer is born again and has a whole new life which wants to take complete control over his daily actions, thoughts, words, attitudes, and motives (2 Corinthians 5:17).

6. Union with Christ

This is the blessing of God to sidestep the power of temptation, our selfishness, and the pull of the world's system. As long as a person is alive to the pressures of the world, their flesh, and the Devil, they will give in. But God connects them to the death of Christ not only for forgiveness of sin but also to allow them to live a new life without the pressures of the old life (Romans 6:1-5). This powerful aspect of salvation is declared to be intimately connected to baptism and the Christian's ability to resist temptation.

7. Adoption

The believer, through salvation, has a new forever family. They have been adopted into God's family and given an inheritance that will not fade away. We are released from the cycles of sin and curses that seek to hold over us our old family allegiances (Galatians 4:3-5; Romans 8:15; John 1:12).

8. Spirit Baptism

God does not leave us alone, when we believe, as individuals trying to fight our way through this world; but He puts us on His team. We become a part of the body of Christ through the baptism of the Holy Spirit when we first believed (1 Corinthians 12:13, Mark 1:8).

9. The Indwelling of the Holy Spirit

God has also not taken up a distant position towards us but is in us directing, guiding, empowering, and ministering through the Holy Spirit that the Lord Jesus sent to be in us (Romans 8:8-11).

10. The Sealing of the Holy Spirit

God puts His mark on His people and they are secure (Ephesians 1:13). God Himself ensures that true believers will be kept from stumbling in a permanent or total fashion (Jude 24).

11. Sanctification

God moves in us and on us constantly to set us apart from those who do not and/or will not believe. He is trying to bless us with a different life -- a life that He has planned for us that is abundant, relational, godly, and Christ-like (Ephesians 2:10; Romans 6:19).

12. The Filling Ministry of the Holy Spirit

When we become Christians, God imbeds His Holy Spirit in our spirits to guide us. His desire is that we will allow Him to flow out of our spirit into our soul and body and let His ideas, directions, wisdom, power, actions, and gifts become the dominant elements in our life (Ephesians 5:18).

13. Spiritual Gifts

One of the most amazing aspects of being saved by the Lord Jesus Christ is that God has given us special abilities to use in specific places for a unique impact which results in the good of others. Each believer has been given at least one of these special abilities that is designed to be used in a specific place for a unique impact. Letting God's power flow through you in this way is a unique ride. (1 Corinthians 12:4-7).

Look over the above 13 aspects of the salvation that God provided in Jesus Christ. Have you understood and taken full advantage of all of these elements of God's way of escape? If not, begin crying out to God to teach you and be prepared to learn.

The future work of God in our lives to complete our salvation

There is far more to the salvation that God provides than the elements which save us from ourselves, others, our sins, and our fate. At some point in the future those who are saved through their faith in the work of God in Jesus will experience the following blessings:

1. Perseverance

God Himself, in various ways and through various means, becomes active in the life of the believer ensuring the completion of the journey of faith (John 10:27-30; Jude 24). Those who have truly been born again will not totally or finally fall away from the faith.

2. Glorification

Also, at some point in the future God becomes uniquely active in the spirit, soul, and body of the believer and purifies as well as glorifies the believer so that they can live in the presence of God (Romans 8:29-30; 1 John 3:2, 3; 1 Thessalonians 5:22,23).

3. Redemption of the Body

For those who died before the return of Christ, the Lord Jesus comes back for the body of those who have died and gives them a new body so that they might be body, soul, and spirit (1 Thessalonians 4:1-8; 1 Corinthians 15:50-58; Romans 8:11).

4. Marriage Supper of the Lamb

God throws a festival to mark the beginning of the completion of His salvation for the faithful. The period of time is often called the marriage supper of the lamb because it is when believers will, for the first time, finally be fully at home with their beloved God. This is the time when the saints shall enjoy the Savior and come to fully appreciate Him in new ways (2 Thessalonians 1:10; Revelation 19:7).

5. New Heavens and New Earth

This is the time to settle into the eternal state, serving the Lord in final glorification in the new heavens and new earth (Revelation 21-22). We shall live in the holy city -- the new Jerusalem -- with all its blessings and wonders; the greatest of which is the Lamb of God which is its light.

The work of God before the world began and your life started to bring you salvation

God was at work before the world began preparing for your salvation the Scriptures tell us (Romans 8:29; Ephesians 1:3,4). It can be very encouraging to see all that God did to bring salvation to us. These are generally considered the major events that took place before God began to bring conviction of sin and His call to faith into our individual lives.

1. God's Foreknowledge

This is the penetrating gaze of God's all-knowing mind which sees everything about the universe before it happens, including all of the possibilities which flow from the choices of mankind (Matthew 11: 21-24; Psalm 139:1-6; Ephesians 1:3,4). Before He brought the universe into being, He knew everything that could happen and everything that would happen.

2. Election

This is the decision of God about who would be saved and who would not be. He made this decision based upon His foreknowledge the Scriptures tell us (Romans 8:28-29; 1 Peter 1:1, 2; Romans 9:14-18). He made His decision based in His goodness, grace, love and wisdom as all that He is in every action and decision He makes (Exodus 34:6,7).

3. Creation of the World

After planning the whole of the universe -- including the allowance of limited freedom of the will to some of His creatures (John 3:16; Joshua 24:15; Genesis 3:6,7), -- God brought the universe into being with its spatial and time dimensions (Genesis 1:1). His purpose seems to be to allow humans to choose to love Him and worship Him (John 4:24).

4. The Fall of Lucifer: The Son of the Morning

Sometime after the creation of the universe and pronouncing it all good (Genesis 1), sin entered into God's perfect creation through the perversion of the highest created being, the angel Lucifer, the anointed cherub that guards. (Ezekiel 28:11-19). He decided he wanted to be like God and rebelled from his appointed position (Isaiah 14:12-16).

5. The Fall of Man

God allowed this rebellious spirit-being, Lucifer, to interact with our first parents, Adam and Eve, to give them a true choice of love or rebellion. Adam and Eve made the same rebellious, selfish choice that Lucifer did and grasped at becoming their own gods. They rebelled from the God-designed submission which would have brought everlasting life and harmony and chose to go their own independent ways. (Genesis 3:1-24).

6. The Establishment of Original Sin

After Adam and Eve rebelled from God, they were immediately stripped of the connection with God that they had been originally created with. They were now alienated from God. They could not pass on to their descendants what they no longer had and the curse of original sin began reaping its deadly toll (Romans 5:12-21).

7. The Incarnation of the God-Man: Jesus The Christ

Before the world was created God knew He would need a Savior for the selfishness and rebelliousness of mankind. The second person of the Trinity, the divine Logos, agreed to become a man and provide salvation. He would pay the penalty for the rebellion and sin of mankind. This God-man then lived a perfect life to meet the requirements for sinlessness and voluntarily gave up His claim on eternal life to take on the sin of the world (1 Corinthians 5:19-21). His endless life as God then allowed Him to offer the sinless perfection of His perfect life to as many as would receive Him (John 1:12).

8. The Restraining Ministry of the Holy Spirit

God also insured that the rebellion and sinfulness of mankind would not become so completely depraved that no one would listen to His conviction and call. God the Holy Spirit was active in the world -- in and through Christians and non-Christians -- of restraining evil. This does not mean that God keeps evil from happening, but that He constantly puts a strain on individuals not to do all the evil that is possible in a given situation (Genesis 6:3; 2 Thessalonians 2:7).

There is wonder in all that God did to bring about salvation for us. Gazing into the mind of God as He planned and executed the universe and our salvation has captivated many people. Stay humble and realize that we have, at best, the roughest outline of what, how, when, and why God did all that He did. God is God and you are not. This topic has caused more than a few to become proud and hostile to those who don't see these elements the way they do.

Spiritual Weapon of Salvation

Spiritual Workout

Make a list of at least three different times when God has given you a way of escape out of a difficulty, temptation, or oppressive situation

1.

2.

3.

Spiritual Workout

Exercises in ways of escape, being rescued, salvation

God will send ways of escape but you must take them!!! The Scripture is clear in 1 Corinthians 10:13 that God will not allow us to be tested without a way of escape, so we do not have to cave into the pressure. The questions are: Are we looking for His ways of escape? Have we begun to believe that His help will never come, and we are on our own? God will send financial, vocational, relational, parental ways of escape that will keep us from giving into temptations that could permanently destroy our lives.

Right now can you pick out the ways of escape that God may be sending in each of your relational arenas? Remember that these ways of escape are to provide you a way of removing yourself from the temptation. But they will not work if you don't take them. Each of these ways of escape are spiritual weapons sent from God.

Spirituality

Marriage/Romance

Family

Work

Church

Finances

Community/Nation

Friends

Enemies

Spiritual Weapon of Salvation

If you keep your eyes open. you will see these ways of escape. But you will also realize that you don't want to take these ways of escape because the temptation is so alluring. The reason why you are hesitating taking the way of escape is because the temptation is attractive to you in some way.

Sometimes it is very helpful to remember the ways that God has delivered us in the past. How has God delivered you in the past? What were the ways of escape that God sent to keep you from a bad relationship, to prevent you from being cheated, to keep you engaged at a crucial time with your kids, to get you to move away from a particular friend?

1.
2.
3.
4.
5.

What ways of escape do you need to take to live a more righteous, loving life? Are there arenas in your life where the testing or temptation is so severe that you don't think you can take it, but you don't see the way of escape? Ask some wise people you know to help you find the way of escape. They may be able to help you see what you cannot see. Who are the people you need to talk to who can help you see the ways of escape?

1.
2.
3.
4.
5.

As you think about the pressures and temptations in your life, where can you reasonably expect God's way of escape to appear?

Personal - Marriage - Family - Vocational - Financial - Church - Society - Friends - Enemies

If you look for them, you will be more able to see them? You may not know what form they will come in but they will come. Circle the above areas where you need a way of escape.

Chapter #7
Spiritual Weapon of the Word of God

The sixth piece of armor is the Word of God. This is also an incredibly powerful spiritual weapon but you must use it. Too many people think of the Bible as some magic book that releases its power just by being physically present in a room. I can remember being asked to go to the home of a couple because their son was seeing spirits that were tormenting him. I began to ask the standard questions about why this might be happening. The couple told me that they were involved in numerous New Age practices, chanting, and meditating under pyramids. When I strongly objected to what they were doing, they told me that it was okay because they had a big family Bible up on the mantle to protect them. I stopped them immediately and grabbed the Bible off their mantle. I said, "This book will do you no good unless you are putting it in you and living by it." They actually believed that a Bible on the shelf was protection against satanic attack when they were calling to demons to come into their home. The words of Scripture had to be unleashed in the lives of believers to release the power in the Word of God. Amazingly, they did not want to read, study, and meditate upon the Scriptures. They wanted me to pray over their son so that he would not see the spirits and shadows that were tormenting him. They wanted the Bible to generate a force field around them and their family so that wicked spirits couldn't plague their son, even while they kept chanting to demons through what they were doing.

I told them that the Bible is a powerful spiritual weapon but only when it is in the life of the believer guiding and producing righteous actions. Without obedience to the concepts, ideas, and righteous actions of the Bible there is no spiritual protection. Contained within the pages of the sacred Scriptures are the ways to defeat every scheme of Satan, but they cannot remain in the pages of a book. They must come to live in the heart and life of the individual. An unopened Bible on a shelf does little to protect against the Devil.

There is something about the words of God spoken by the believer that cuts through the lies, fear, and fog of the Devil. Let's take a look at how this weapon of the Word of God was used by Jesus and the other heroes of the faith in the Bible. (Notice how in each of these cases the Scripture is quoted, contemplated, or heard.)

> *Then Jesus was led up by the Spirit into the wilderness to be tempted by the devil. And after He had fasted forty days and forty nights, He then became hungry. And the tempter came and said to Him, "If You are the Son of God, command that these stones become bread." But He answered and said, "It is written, 'MAN SHALL NOT LIVE ON BREAD ALONE, BUT ON EVERY WORD THAT PROCEEDS OUT OF THE MOUTH OF GOD.'" Then the devil took Him into the holy city and had Him stand on the pinnacle of the temple, and said to Him, "If You are the Son of God, throw Yourself down; for it is written, 'HE WILL COMMAND HIS ANGELS CONCERNING YOU'; and 'ON their HANDS THEY WILL BEAR YOU UP, SO THAT YOU WILL NOT STRIKE YOUR FOOT*

Spiritual Weapon of the Word of God

> *AGAINST A STONE.'" Jesus said to him, "On the other hand, it is written, 'YOU SHALL NOT PUT THE LORD YOUR GOD TO THE TEST.'" Again, the devil took Him to a very high mountain and showed Him all the kingdoms of the world and their glory; and he said to Him, "All these things I will give You, if You fall down and worship me." Then Jesus said to him, "Go, Satan! For it is written, 'YOU SHALL WORSHIP THE LORD YOUR GOD, AND SERVE HIM ONLY.'" Then the devil left Him; and behold, angels came and began to minister to Him.* Matthew 4:4

In Matthew 16:15 Simon Peter heard a word from God about who Jesus was and he spoke it out. This is what God wants His children to do to defeat the Devil. It is important to realize that just a few minutes later Peter seemed to feel that whatever he thought was inspired, and so he tried to tell the Lord that He didn't have to die. Jesus rebuked him for being used by the Devil. Be clear when God puts a word of Scripture on your heart. Don't just say what you think.

> *He said to them, "But who do you say that I am?" Simon Peter answered, "You are the Christ, the Son of the Living God." And Jesus said to him, "Blessed are you Simon Barjona, because flesh and blood did not reveal this to you, but My Father who is in heaven. I also say to you that you are Peter and upon this rock I will build My church; and the gates of Hades will not overpower it."* Matthew 16:15

In Matthew 10:25-27 the Lord tells the disciples that they will need to speak the Word of God that they hear whispered in their ears. He is saying that God will prompt them with His words. Expect that He will direct you.

If they have called the head of the house Beelzebul, how much more will they malign the members of his household? Therefore do not fear them, for there is nothing concealed that will not be revealed, or hidden that will not be known. <u>What I tell you in the darkness, speak in the light,</u> and <u>what you hear whispered in your ear, proclaim upon the housetops.</u> Do not fear those who kill the body but are unable to kill the soul; but rather fear Him who is able to destroy both body and soul in hell. Matthew 10:25-27

One of the forgotten truths about hearing the Word of God when He prompts is you need to know the Word of God at some level, or you will not be able to hear or understand what God is saying. God prompts and guides us through the truth, stories, principles, and judgments of the Scriptures.

<u>Let the word of Christ richly dwell within you</u> with all wisdom teaching and admonishing one another with psalms and hymns and spiritual songs, singing with thankfulness in your hearts to God. Colossians 3:16

The Apostle Peter declares that we desire to draw in the Word of God and only when it is in us will we be nourished by it and guided by it. We live in a world full of malice, deceit, and slander which is very corrupting. We need to detoxify from these things through taking in the Word of God. The Word of God will fill and reorganize our souls. When you are abiding in the Word, you do not know what God will say; but you will hear and understand more of it when you are familiar with the Bible.

Spiritual Weapon of the Word of God

Therefore, putting aside all malice and all deceit and hypocrisy and envy and all slander, like newborn babies, <u>long for the pure milk of the word, so that by it you may grow in respect to salvation</u>, if you have tasted of the kindness of the Lord. 1 Peter 2:1-3

God brings a particular Scripture to mind that will counteract the thought, temptation, or manipulation of the Devil. It is this particular passage that needs to be noticed and repeated until it gives clarity in the situation. The Apostle Paul is helping us understand that the whispered Scriptures will make a significant difference in the life and choices of the believer. This is not just about having a Bible or even reading the Bible. This is about having the words of the Bible in you so that the Holy Spirit can bring to your remembrance just the right Scripture that you need to defeat Satan.

The Greek word used in Ephesians 6 translated "word" is *rhema,* which means "spoken word." The Apostle Paul seems to be making a distinction between the written Word of God (logos) contained in the written Scriptures and the Word of God whispered by the Holy Spirit to the believer in the midst of battle and spoken out by those who believe and trust Him. When Satan seduces, tempts, and pressures the believer, the believer must have hidden God's Word in his mind so that the Holy Spirit can whisper the Word to his heart and can then speak it out like thrusts into the Devil's side. This is just as the Lord Jesus did in His temptation in Matthew 4. When a believer is facing a satanic scheme, we wait for a word from the Lord that we can use to defeat that particular plot of the Devil. This assumes that we have spent time in the written Word of God (logos) so He can bring to mind the Word (rhema) when it is needed. The Word of God is a powerful tool when it is in the mouth and life of His servants. It is of no value when it is left unknown and unused on printed pages.

The Psalmist echoes a similar sentiment when he says, *"Your Word I have treasured in my heart that I may not sin against You"* (Psalm 119:11).

Much of the early church's discipleship was built around memorization of and/or slow repetition of five key passages of Scripture: The Lord's Prayer; The Great Commandments and The Ten Commandments; The Beatitudes; The Ladder of Virtue/Fruit of the Spirit; plus the Apostles Creed. These passages of Scripture give the Spirit of Christ the crucial ideas, boundaries, and phrases to guide any believer in the way they should go (Isaiah 55:3). Listening for God to whisper these verses, phrases, and ideas in your soul is so powerful. These passages were the beginning point in following the Lord. Each of these passages were meditated upon and explained in detail and thorough questioning (catechism). It was understood that if the average Christian had a working understanding of these concepts, ideas, and phrases, they would basically be mature and ready for the challenges of the Christian life. I find tremendous benefit in saying all of these passages every day. These passages ground me in God's moral and spiritual universe. Other Scriptures can also be committed to memory as the believer continues to grow in their faith. Just read through the following passages slowly at least three times today (breakfast, lunch, and dinner). Let your lips say these words either softly or loudly and let your soul be bathed in the truths of these words.

The Beatitudes
Matthew 5:3-12

Blessed are the poor in spirit, for theirs is the kingdom of heaven.
Blessed are those who mourn, for they shall be comforted.
Blessed are the gentle, for they shall inherit the earth.
Blessed are those who hunger and thirst for righteousness, for they shall be satisfied.
Blessed are the merciful, for they shall receive mercy.
Blessed are the pure in heart, for they shall see God.
Blessed are the peacemakers, for they shall be called sons of God.
Blessed are those who have been persecuted for the sake of righteousness, for theirs is the kingdom of heaven.
Blessed are you when men cast insults at you, and persecute you, and say all kinds of evil against you falsely, on account of Me. Rejoice, and be glad, for your reward in heaven is great, for so they persecuted the prophets who were before you.

The Two Great Commandments
Matthew 22:37-39

You shall love the Lord your God with all your heart, soul, mind and strength
and your neighbor as yourself.

The Ten Commandments
Exodus 20:1-17

1 THEN God spoke all these words, saying,
2 I am the LORD your God, who brought you out of the land of Egypt, out of the house of slavery.
3 You shall have no other gods before Me.
4 You shall not make for yourself an idol, or any likeness of what is in heaven above or on the earth beneath or in the water under the earth.
5 You shall not worship them or serve them; for I, the LORD your God, am a jealous God, visiting the iniquity of the fathers on the children, on the third and the fourth generations of those who hate Me,
6 but showing lovingkindness to thousands, to those who love Me and keep My commandments.
7 You shall not take the name of the LORD your God in vain, for the LORD will not leave him unpunished who takes His name in vain.
8 Remember the Sabbath day, to keep it holy.
9 Six days you shall labor and do all your work, 10 but the seventh day is a sabbath of the LORD your God; in it you shall not do any work, you or your son or your daughter, your male or your female servant or your cattle or your sojourner who stays with you.
11 For in six days the LORD made the heavens and the earth, the sea and all that is in them, and rested on the seventh day; therefore the LORD blessed the sabbath day and made it holy.
12 Honor your father and your mother, that your days may be prolonged in the land which the LORD your God gives you.
13 You shall not murder.
14 You shall not commit adultery.
15 You shall not steal.
16 You shall not bear false witness against your neighbor.

17 You shall not covet your neighbor's house; you shall not covet your neighbor's wife or his male servant or his female servant or his ox or his donkey or anything that belongs to your neighbor.

The Lord's Prayer
Matthew 6:9-13

9 Pray, then, in this way:
Our Father who is in heaven,
Hallowed be Your name.
10 Your kingdom come.
Your will be done,
On earth as it is in heaven.
11 Give us this day our daily bread.
12 And forgive us our debts, as we also have forgiven our debtors.
13 And do not lead us into temptation, but deliver us from evil. For Yours is the kingdom, and the power, and the glory, forever. Amen.

The Ladder of Virtue
2 Peter 1:5-11

Now for this very reason also, applying all diligence, in your faith supply moral excellence, and in your moral excellence, knowledge; and in your knowledge, self-control, and in your self-control, perseverance, and in your perseverance, godliness; and in your godliness, brotherly kindness, and in your brotherly kindness, love. For if these qualities are yours and are increasing, they render you neither useless nor unfruitful in the true knowledge of our Lord Jesus Christ. For he who lacks these qualities is blind or short-sighted, having forgotten his purification from his former sins. Therefore, brethren, be all the more diligent to make certain about His calling and choosing you; for as long as you practice these things, you will never stumble; for in this way the entrance into the eternal kingdom of our Lord and Savior Jesus Christ will be abundantly supplied to you.

The Fruit of the Spirit

Galatians 5:22,23

But the fruit of the Spirit is love, joy, peace, patience, kindness, goodness, faithfulness, gentleness, self-control; against such things there is no law.

Become a person of the Word of God so that the Author of the Word can speak to you!

Spiritual Weapon of the Word of God

Spiritual Workout

The Word of God exercises

God is whispering in your soul the guidance and direction you need to defeat the work of the Devil. The way that He does this is through the Scriptures. The more of the Scriptures you know, the more clear the guidance of God will be. The Devil is always trying to redirect your life so as to damage or destroy your relationships.

One of the most life-changing exercises that I have ever assigned is to ask God for guidance through the Proverbs and Psalms.

Write out or think of the number one problem you are facing and read through the proverb for that day, looking for God's guidance on that issue. The proverb for the day is the chapter of Proverbs that corresponds to that day. Read the 15th chapter of Proverbs on the 15th. Read through the proverb with that problem or practical question on your mind. God will begin to highlight verses that are His guidance on that issue. You can also keep reading prayerfully through the Psalms, starting with the chapter in the Psalms that corresponds to the day of the month it is. To increase your search through Psalms, read five chapters of Psalms and not just one. If it is the 15th of the month read the 15th Proverb, the 15th Psalm and then the 45th Psalm, the 75th Psalm, the 105th Psalm and the 135th Psalm. The idea is to add thirty to the original Psalm four times and you will get a broader picture of God's wisdom on the topic you are prayerfully bringing to God.

Let me give you a brief overview of how to biblically meditate on a verse and allow God to guide you.

First, pick a verse that corresponds to the issue or problem you are having. The following are a few suggested verses:

Scriptures	Problems or Issue
James 1:19	Anger, gossip, pride
Ephesians 5:25	Marriage improvement
Proverbs 18:1	Divorce, big decisions
Romans 12:1,2	Temptation, loving God
Philippians 4:6-8	Worry, movie guide, thought life
Romans 6:1-12	Temptation, Christ's power
Colossians 3:12-15	Positive qualities, living each day
1 John 1:5-2:2	Getting rid of sin, forgiveness
Exodus 20:3-17	Ten Commandments, right & wrong
Proverbs 15:1-4	Calming anger, speaking well
Ephesians 1:18-21	Christian power and prestige
Ephesians 3:14-21	Love, strengthened with power
Matthew 5:3-12	How to be like Christ, how to act
Galatians 5:22,23	What God will prompt you to do

Spiritual Weapon of the Word of God

Relationship	Scriptures
God	Philippians 3:14-16; John 17:1-5; Matthew 6:1-4; Revelation 2:2-5
Self	Ephesians 4:30-32; Matthew 5:21-26; Proverbs 6:16-19; 1 Peter 4:7-11
Marriage	Ephesians 5:22-30; 1 Peter 3:7; Genesis 2:18-25; Matthew 22:22-30
Family	1 Timothy 3:4,5; Ephesians 6:1-3; Psalm 127:1-5; Matthew 10:34-39
Work	Colossians 3:22-24; Proverbs 21:5,6; 1 Corinthians 15:58; 2 Thessalonians 3:7-11
Church	Hebrews 10:22-25; 1 Corinthians 12:12-17; Matthew 16:18,19; 1 Corinthians 5:9-13
Money	Matthew 6:19-24; Proverbs 27:23-27; 1 Timothy 6:7-10; Romans 13:5-8
Society	Exodus 20:3-17; 1 Timothy 1:8-11; 1 Timothy 2:1-7
Friends	Proverbs 11:13; 17:9; 17:17; 18:24; 22:24-27; 27:6

Doctrinal Category	Scriptures
Bible	John 17:17; 2 Timothy 3:16
God	Psalm 90:2; Isaiah 40:18; Isaiah 44:6b; 45:21,22
Christ	John 1:29; Philippians 2:5-11; John 1:1-3,14
Holy Spirit	Acts 5:3,4; Acts 1:8; John 14:16; 1 John 2:27
Salvation	Romans 1:18; 2 Corinthians 5:17,21; John 6:29; Romans 10:9,10
Man	Jeremiah 17:9; 1 Thessalonians 5:23; Hebrews 2:6-8
Church	Matthew 16:17; Colossians 1:18; Galatians 6:1-10
Angels	Hebrews 1:14; 13:2; Job 1
Heaven, Hell, & Judgment Day	Revelation 22:1-3; John 14:3; Luke 16: 23; Revelation 20:15; Romans 8:11
Christ's Return	Philippians 3:20,21; 1 Thessalonians 4:13-18

Second, slowly repeat the verse over and over throughout the day. Emphasize different words and different phrases. Think about what this verse is really saying about your issue, problem, or difficulty. It may be coming at the problem from a completely different angle.

Third, take some time to study the verse by writing it out on a separate piece of paper, circling key words you want to look up, noticing transitions from one thought to another, asking questions that come to your mind about the verse, looking up the words in a dictionary, looking at cross references that will help you understand the verse, reading other translations of the verse, trying and answering the questions you asked, look at commentaries, asking God what He wants you to know, feel, or do because of what this verse says.

Fourth, personalize the verse by putting your name or personal pronouns in the verse where you can. Aim the verse right at yourself.

Fifth, confess the truths in the verse. Are there things in the verse that are true of you? Thank God for the fact that you are doing good on those things. Are there things in the verse that you are not doing well? Confess those to God and ask that He give you new energy to make a different choice next time.

Sixth, visualize the verse. See yourself living out the truths, actions, or speech that are in the verse. Mentally rehearse yourself doing the actions of the verse.

Seventh, diagram or develop metaphors for the truths in the verse. Make a diagram of doing the verse so that the truths, steps, blessings, or consequences of those are clearly seen. Some may want to write metaphors or analogies of the truths or actions of the verse.

Eighth, pray the truths, feelings, actions in the verse. Ask God for everything in the verse. Talk to God about everything in the verse, even if some is confusing.

Ninth, sing the verse. Add any melody under the verse and just enjoy the process of singing the word of God.

Tenth, journal or record the insights that you gain by spending this much time on one verse. The more you notice the insights that God gives you, the more He will give you.

Eleventh, write your own translation of the verse. This should take into account all that you have learned and understood about the verse.

If you will apply the above method to the verses that deal with the issues of your life, you will be amazed at how God's guidance and energy will allow you to change your life in a positive direction.

Spiritual Weapon of the Word of God

Spiritual Workout

Biblical Affirmations

Let me tell you some of the biblically-based affirmations that I say every day to help me picture and stay on track to the righteous life I want and I know God wants for me. Because I say these every day, I am constantly alerted to ways to make these wonderful relationships happen. I usually say them in the morning.

> Every day I have an encounter with God that fills me with love, guidance, wisdom, and power.
>
> Every day I enjoy a relationship with my wife of hilarious love, deep comfortability, full acceptance, godly priorities, expanding intimacy.
>
> Every week I delight in a great relationship with my girls through the 6 R's: Respect, Relationship, Responsibility, Rules, Rituals, and Resources.
>
> I have a full network of acquaintances, casual friends, close friends, and intimate friends, who help me promote and live a vibrant Christian life.
>
> Every month I am abundantly supplied by God financially through work, savings, investments, and businesses.
>
> Quote Scripture that comes to mind when you are facing excessive worry, fear, anger, hatred, temptation. Keep quoting it under your breath until the internal feelings or desires pass.

Chapter #8
Spiritual Weapon of Prayer

The weapon of prayer is often overlooked in discussions of God's Armor because it is not couched in the metaphor of a Roman soldier's armor. However, prayer is one of the most important spiritual weapons the believer can possess in warfare with Satan. Unfortunately the average Christian is used to praying weak, ineffective prayers. Satan is unaffected by this type of prayer. Prayer as a weapon in the warfare with Satan must be specific, doctrinal, and based on the Holy Spirit's promptings. A nonspecific prayer for traveling mercies will not accomplish much in the battle. In his two books, *The Adversary* and *Overcoming the Adversary,* Mark Bubeck provides help in explaining and rediscovering effective praying in a demonic context. These books and their prayers are quite helpful for all Christians. When average Christians learn to pray in this powerful way, they are released like tigers into the battle. I have seen mild-mannered and somewhat meek individuals transformed into great spiritual warriors through prayers of this nature.

Look at how Jesus and the heroes of the faith used prayer in the midst of spiritual battle. In this first reference, Jesus rebukes the disciples because they were clearly not praying in the midst of the demonic encounter.

And Jesus rebuked him, and the demon came out of him, and the boy was cured at once. Then the disciples came to Jesus privately and said, "Why could we not drive it

out? And He said to them, "Because of the littleness of your faith; for truly I say to you, if you have faith the size of a mustard seed, you will say to this mountain, 'Move from here to there,' and it will move; and nothing will be impossible to you. <u>But this kind does not go out except by prayer and fasting.</u>"
Matthew 17:18-21

They must have just launched into their deliverance routines without seeking God's direction and power in prayer. They most likely had performed deliverances in the past based upon the authority that Jesus gave them and it had become routine. Jesus basically says that they needed further instructions from God if they were going to deliver the boy from the kind of demon that they were facing.

One of the most instructive spiritual warfare prayers we have is the one between God the Son and God the Father in the midst of the most intense spiritual battle in the history of the world. Would Jesus voluntarily choose to lay down His life and pay for the sins of the world? It is clear in the prayer and in the other accounts in the Gospels that it was a real battle.

Jesus spoke these things; and lifting up His eyes to heaven, He said, "Father, the hour has come; glorify Your Son, that the Son may glorify You, even as You gave Him authority over all flesh, that to all whom You have given Him, He may give eternal life. This is eternal life, that they may know You, the only true God, and Jesus Christ whom You have sent. I glorified You on the earth, having accomplished the work which You have given Me to do. Now, Father, glorify Me together with Yourself, with the glory which I had with You before the world was. I have manifested Your name to the men whom You gave Me out of the world; they were Yours and You gave them to Me, and they have kept Your word. Now they have come to know that everything You have given Me is from You; for the words which You gave Me I have given to them; and they received them and truly understood that I came forth from You, and they believed that You sent Me. I ask on their behalf; I do not ask on behalf of the world, but of those whom You have given Me; for they are Yours; and all things that are Mine are Yours, and Yours are Mine; and I have been glorified in them. I am no longer in the world; and yet they themselves are in the world, and I come to You. Holy Father, keep them in Your name, the name which You have given Me, that they may be one even as We are. While I was with them, I was keeping them in Your name which You have given Me; and I guarded them and not one of them perished but the son of perdition, so that the Scripture would be fulfilled. But now I come to You; and these things I speak in the world so that they may have My joy made full in themselves. I have given them Your word; and the world has hated them, because they are not of the world, even as I am not of the world. I do not ask You to take them out of the world, but to keep them from the evil one. They are not of the world, even as I am not of the world. Sanctify them in the truth; Your word is truth. As You sent Me into the world, I also have sent them into the world. For their sakes I sanctify Myself, that they themselves also may be sanctified in truth. I do not ask on behalf of these alone, but for those also who believe in Me through their word; that they may all be one; even as You, Father, are in Me and I in You, that they also may be in Us, so that the world may believe that You sent Me. The glory which You have given Me I *have given to them, that they may be one, just as We are one; I in them and You in Me, that they may be perfected in unity, so that the world may know that You sent Me, and loved them, even as You have loved Me. Father, I desire that they also, whom You have given Me, be with Me where I am, so that they may see My glory which You have given Me, for You loved Me before the foundation of the world. O righteous Father, although the world has not known You, yet I have known You; and these have known that You sent Me; and I have made Your name known to them, and will make it known, so that the love with which You loved Me may be in them, and I in them."* John 17:1

The tenderness of the prayer, the confidence, the looking to the future, and the relationship between Father and Son is what makes this prayer so dynamic. This prayer creates spiritual space for Jesus' decision: "Not as I will, but as You will."

I have included another look at the spiritual battle in the Garden of Gethsemane and how prayer won the day.

Then Jesus came with them to a place called Gethsemane, and said to His disciples, "Sit here while I go over there and pray." And He took with Him Peter and the two sons of Zebedee, and began to be grieved and distressed. Then He said to them, "My soul is deeply grieved, to the point of death; remain here and keep watch with Me." And He went a little beyond them, and fell on His face and prayed, saying, "My Father, if it is possible, let this cup pass from Me; yet not as I will, but as You will." And He came to the disciples and found them sleeping, and said to Peter,

Spiritual Weapon of Prayer

> *"So, you men could not keep watch with Me for one hour? <u>Keep watching and praying that you may not enter into temptation; the spirit is willing, but the flesh is weak.</u>" He went away again <u>a second time and prayed, saying</u>, "My Father, if this cannot pass away unless I drink it, Your will be done." Again He came and found them sleeping, for their eyes were heavy. And He left them again, <u>and went away and prayed a third time,</u> saying the same thing once more. Then He came to the disciples and said to them, "Are you still sleeping and resting? Behold, the hour is at hand and the Son of Man is being betrayed into the hands of sinners. Get up, let us be going; behold, the one who betrays Me is at hand!"* Matthew 26:36-46

Many people want to short circuit the drama of this prayer by saying that Jesus had to do it. Don't let your theological philosophy keep you from seeing the reality of the spiritual warfare.

Notice in this next use of prayer as a spiritual weapon that the angel Michael does not directly challenge the Devil but instead prays and rebukes him. He stays under the authority of the Lord Jesus.

> *But Michael the archangel, when he disputed with the devil and argued about the body of Moses, did not dare pronounce against him a railing judgment, but said, "<u>The Lord rebuke you!</u>"* Jude 9

There is often too much pride, posturing, and ego power in spiritual warfare episodes. There is a need for the kind of humility and dependence that Michael shows here.

When used properly, prayer can create a climate of liberty and freedom. Prayer by the leaders of a church can protect the church and dilute the satanic outrage involved in exposing his strategies. Prayer by the leaders can sensitize them for the specific direction that God may give during the conference. In the church I served, I went through four major upheavals in a few years and many families left. While the surface causes were different in every case, each came at a time of intensive teaching on spiritual warfare without adequate prayer by the leadership of the church. I realized that I needed to pray much more and the leadership must pray at a new level if we were going to expose what Satan was doing.

Actual Warfare Prayers

I have included two warfare prayers that I regularly pray and have others pray. The first one is what I pray before I go to bed every night in order to protect my family and myself. The second one is what I pray for people who are struggling with significant demonic influence. Many people who are facing significant demonic influence cannot pray the second prayer for themselves at the beginning. They need you to pray it for them.

Spiritual Workout

Prayer before bed

Dear Heavenly Father,

I come to you in the name of the Lord Jesus Christ. I thank you for all you have done for me. I ask that you would protect my wife, my children, and myself in every part of who we are. Please place our spirit, soul, and body under the protection that comes from the blood of Jesus Christ and the power of the Holy Spirit. I ask that you would not allow the Devil to attack or disturb us while we sleep or during the day tomorrow. Please, Lord Jesus, minister to us as we sleep and go about our business tomorrow.

In the Name of the Lord Jesus Christ,
Amen

Spiritual Workout

I have used the following prayer in all kinds of situations to pray very strong truth, righteousness, and faith into a situation. I have prayed this for others, and I have prayed this prayer for myself. I have various versions of this type of prayer that I have authored, but I love to go back to Mark Bubeck's version from his wonderful book, *The Adversary*.

Prayer of Warfare

"Heavenly Father, I bow in worship and praise before You. I cover myself with the blood of the Lord Jesus Christ as my protection during this time of prayer. I surrender myself completely and unreservedly in every area of my life to Yourself. I do take a stand against all the workings of Satan that would hinder me in this time of prayer, and I address myself only to the true and living God and refuse any involvement of Satan in my prayer."

"Satan, I command you, in the name of the Lord Jesus Christ, to leave my presence with all your demons, and I bring the blood of the Lord Jesus Christ between us. Heavenly Father, I worship You, and I give You praise. I recognize that You are worthy to receive all glory and honor and praise. I renew my allegiance to You and pray that the blessed Holy Spirit would enable me in

this time of prayer. I am thankful, Heavenly Father, that You have loved me from past eternity, that You sent the Lord Jesus Christ into the world to die as my substitute that I would be redeemed. I am thankful that the Lord Jesus Christ came as my representative and that through him You have completely forgiven me; You have given me eternal life; You have given me the perfect righteousness of the Lord Jesus Christ, so I am now justified. I am thankful that in Him You have made me complete, and that You have offered Yourself to me to be my daily help and strength."

"Heavenly Father, come and open my eyes that I might see how great You are and how complete Your provision is for this new day. I do, in the name of the Lord Jesus Christ, take my place with Christ in the heavenlies with all principalities and powers (powers of darkness and wicked spirits) under my feet. I am thankful that the victory the Lord Jesus Christ is in the heavenlies; therefore, I declare that all principalities and powers and all wicked spirits are subject to me in the name of the Lord Jesus Christ."

"I am thankful for the armor You have provided, and I put on the girdle of truth, the breastplate of righteousness, the sandals of peace, and the helmet of salvation. I lift up the shield of faith against all the fiery darts of the Enemy, and take in my hand the sword of the spirit, the Word of God. I use Your Word against all the forces of evil in my life, and I put on this armor and live and pray in complete dependence upon You, blessed Holy Spirit."

"I am grateful, Heavenly Father, that the Lord Jesus Christ spoiled all the principalities and powers and made a show of them openly and triumphed over them in Himself. I claim all that victory for my life today. I reject out of my life all the insinuations, the accusations, and the temptations of Satan. I

affirm that the Word of God is true, and I choose to live today in the light of God's Word. I choose, Heavenly Father, to live in obedience to You and in fellowship with Yourself. Open my eyes and show me the areas of my life that would not please You. Work in my life that there be no ground to give Satan a foothold against me. Show me any area of weakness. Show me any area of my life that I must deal with so that I would please You. I do in every way today stand for You and the ministry of the Holy Spirit in my life."

"By faith and in dependence upon You, I put off the old man and stand in all the victory of the crucifixion where the Lord Jesus Christ provided cleansing from the old nature. I put on the new man and stand into all the victory of the resurrection and the provision He has made for me there to live above sin. Therefore, in this day, I put off the old nature with its selfishness, and I put on the new nature with its love. I put off the old nature with its fear and I put on the new nature with its strength. I put off today the old nature with all its deceitful lusts and I put on the new nature with all its righteousness and purity."

"I do in every way stand in the victory of the ascension and the glorification of the Son of God where all principalities and powers were made subject to Him I claim my place in Christ victorious with Him over all the enemies of my soul. Blessed Holy Spirit, I pray that You would fill me. Come into my life, and break down every idol. Cast out every foe."

"I am thankful, Heavenly Father, for the expression of your will for my daily life as You have shown me in Your Word. I therefore claim all the will of God for today. I am thankful that You have blessed me with all spiritual blessings in heavenly places in Christ Jesus. I am thankful that You have begotten me unto a living hope by the resurrection of Jesus Christ from the dead. I am thankful that You have made a provision so that today I can live filled with the Spirit of God with love and joy and self-control in my life. I recognize that this is Your will for me, and I therefore reject and resist all the endeavors of Satan and of his demons to rob me of the will of God."

"I refuse in this day to believe my feelings, and I hold up the shield of faith against all the accusations and against all the insinuations that Satan would put in my mind. I claim the fullness of the will of God for today."

"I do, in the name of the Lord Jesus Christ, completely surrender myself to You, Heavenly Father, as a living sacrifice. I choose not to be conformed to this world. I choose to be transformed by the renewing of my mind, and I pray that You would show me Your will and enable me to walk in all the fullness of the will of God today."

"I am thankful, Heavenly Father, that the weapons of our warfare are not carnal, but mighty through God to the pulling down of strongholds, to casting down of imaginations and every high thing that exalted itself against the knowledge of God, and to bring every thought into obedience to the Lord Jesus Christ. Therefore in my own life today I tear down the strongholds of Satan, and I smash the plans of Satan that have been formed against me. I tear down the strongholds of Satan against my mind, and I surrender my mind to You, blessed Holy Spirit. I affirm, Heavenly Father, that You have not given us the spirit of fear, but of power and of love and of a sound mind. I break and smash the strongholds of Satan formed against my emotions today, and I give my emotions to You. I smash the strongholds of Satan formed against my will today and I give my will to You, and choose to make the right decisions of faith. I smash the strongholds of Satan formed against my body today, and I give *my body to You, recognizing that I am Your temple; and I rejoice in Your mercy and Your goodness."*

"Heavenly Father, I pray that now through this day You would quicken me; show me the way that Satan is hindering, tempting, lying, counterfeiting, and distorting the truth in my life. Enable me to be the kind of person that would please You. Enable me to be aggressive in prayer. Enable me to be aggressive mentally and to think Your thoughts after You, and to give You Your rightful place in my life."

"Again, I now cover myself with the blood of the Lord Jesus Christ and pray that You, blessed Holy Spirit, would bring all the work of the crucifixion, all the work of the resurrection, all the work of the glorification, and all the work of Pentecost in to my life today. I surrender myself to You. I refuse to be discouraged. You are God of all hope. You have proven Your power by resurrecting Jesus Christ from the dead, and I claim in every way Your victory over all satanic forces active in my life, and I reject these forces; and I pray in the name of the Lord Jesus Christ with thanksgiving. Amen."[1]

---

[1] Bubeck, Mark, *The Adversary*. (Moody Press, 2013), pp. 141-144.

Spiritual Workout

Prayer Exercises

One of the great dangers of Spiritual Warfare is it is about being free of demonic influence, but the person doesn't take new ground in their life. They don't go anywhere new with their freedom. This is not the way it should be. Christ sets us free to live a wonderful life of love and radiating His glory. Your freedom from demonic influence must thrust you to new relationships, new places, new skills, new principles. In fact you are not really free until you go to the places, relationships, and skills that God has planned for you. Don't be let out of your demonic cell and then stay in the prison. Escape from the stronghold of the Devil (built through fear, doubt, sin, selfishness, and lies) and push on to a new life full of answered prayer and God's enabling grace.

We glorify Christ and beat back the Devil when we do the good works that He has designed for us to do (Ephesians 2:10). God wants us to live a righteous life, maximally demonstrating Christ through the gifts, abilities and opportunities that He will bring to us. Our goal should be to accomplish as many of these as we can. It will require His guidance, energy, ability, and gifts to accomplish this. Let's talk specifically about particular ways of swinging the spiritual weapon of prayer.

God wants to fulfill your righteous desires

One of the amazing truths that God has shared with us in the Scriptures is that He wants to support us, bless us, and build a great life for us. But we must stay in contact with Him to get there. Some have tried to incrust this truth of God's desire to bless us with all kinds of crass, materialistic, and even selfish elements, which is a distortion. But look at these verses of

Scripture, read them over slowly, and meditate upon them. These are only a few of the verses that state plainly that God wants to fulfill our righteous desires. I believe that many of us are asking God for far too little. One of the greatest ways to push back the Devil is to begin to fully ask God to use us to fulfill the dreams that He had for us and that He put within us.

Psalms 37:4 - *Delight yourself in the Lord and He will give you the desires of your heart.*

Matthew 5:14-16 - *You are the light of the world. A city set on a hill cannot be hidden... Let our light shine before men in such a way that they may see your good works, and glorify your Father who is in heaven.*

John 10:10b - *I came that they might have life and mighty have it abundantly.*

2 Chronicles 16:9 - *The eyes of the Lord move to and fro across the whole earth to strongly support those whose heart is completely His.*

Since life is relationships at its core, then it would be helpful to have you look at each relationship and begin to describe the righteous ideal in that relationship. I have found that it is helpful if you look out five years from now and try and describe the ideal relationship. You don't have to know how you are going to get there. In fact, that is why I was counseled to look out five years because your need for "the how" can shut off when you are looking out that far into the future. This level of connection to God in prayer can radically revolutionize your life and allow you to be a completely different person five years from now as Christ transforms you relationally.

Let me give a crucial disclaimer. God is not interested in fulfilling your selfish, evil, materialistic desires. God wants to fulfill your righteous desires. When you begin asking Him to fulfill through you the two great commandments -- Love God, love others, and righteously love yourself -- then He is all over it. He does not want you to harm others. If your getting what you desire would harm others, then you should not have it. And He will not be involved in your getting it. But if you will reach out and trust Him in new ways to build a loving life, then He will strongly support that and bring toward you that which you need to accomplish these righteous goals.

In each relationship of life what would the ideal life look like in five years from now if God were to give it to you? I will usually get a legal pad and put each relationship at the top of a blank sheet of paper and then start writing what the ideal relationship in that arena would look like five years from now. I note how old I will be. How old the other person will be. What they and/or I may be interested in at that point in our lives. Where we may be living or working at the time in this ideal world. I will often carry this legal pad around with me for three months and just keep adding to it. I also have a notes page on my phone like this for each relationship, so I can jot things down whenever.

I have put God and Spirituality first but for many people it is the hardest to describe, so you can skip over it and come back to it as the other relationships start to flow. I usually suggest thinking about your relationship with God in terms of the level of guidance and wisdom you are receiving from Him. Also, the practice of the spiritual disciplines has been the typical way to increase one's spiritual relationship with God. I have also put money in as a major relationship. Some have objected to money as a key relationship. But I point out that in Matthew 6, Jesus states that money is the only thing that is so powerful that it can rival God, and we do have a relationship with it. Our job is to master our relationship with money so well that we keep it a thing and do not let it become more and especially not a God. I have only put ten slots under each heading to get you started, but this list may grow to 25 to 100 under each relationship. It will also change over the time you prayerfully and critically examine your list.

If life were ideal in your relationship with God (spirituality), in five years what would that relationship be like?

1.

2.

3.

4.

5.

6.

7.

8.

9.

10.

If life were ideal in your relationship with Self (Body, Soul, Spirit), in five years what would that relationship be like?

1.

2.

3.

4.

5.

6.

7.

8.

9.

10.

Spiritual Weapon of Prayer

If life were ideal in your relationship with Marriage (Romance/Affection), in five years what would that relationship be like?

1.

2.

3.

4.

5.

6.

7.

8.

9.

10.

If life were ideal in your relationship with Family (Immediate/Extended), in five years what would that relationship be like?

1.

2.

3.

4.

5.

6.

7.

8.

9.

10.

If life were ideal in your relationship with Work (Boss/Colleagues), in five years what would that relationship be like?

1.

2.

3.

4.

5.

6.

7.

8.

9.

10.

If life were ideal in your relationship with Church (Leaders/Friends), in five years what would that relationship be like?

1.

2.

3.

4.

5.

6.

7.

8.

9.

10.

If life were ideal in your relationship with Friends (Old/New), in five years what would that relationship be like?

1.

2.

3.

4.

5.

6.

7.

8.

9.

10.

If life were ideal in your relationship with Money (Income/Savings), in five years what would that relationship be like?

1.

2.

3.

4.

5.

6.

7.

8.

9.

10.

If life were ideal in your relationship with Community (Local/National), in five years what would that relationship be like?

1.

2.

3.

4.

5.

6.

7.

8.

9.

10.

If life were ideal in your relationship with Enemies (Past/Current), in five years what would that relationship be like?

1.

2.

3.

4.

5.

6.

7.

8.

9.

10.

I have also had the privilege of taking my wife and my daughters through this exercise for them. It is delightful to see how they are being led by God and what they are thinking. I would ask these questions, and I would just write down what they said. This has been a wonderful and affirming exercise as they build and trust God at new levels. As they embrace this spiritual truth of God's desire to strongly support us, it will light their way just as it has been a light, sword, and shield to me.

Spiritual Weapon of Prayer

Spiritual Workout

Specific Prayer Exercises

Prayer is communication with God about what you specifically need for your life. Plead with God to send what you need specifically in order to live a righteous, God- honoring life.

What answers, guidance, or blessings from God do you need to live a righteous, loving, supremely successful life in each relational category? If you were to get on the phone and call God right now, what help, guidance, and discussions would you have with Him? Have that conversation right now.

God (Answers, Guidance, Blessings)

Self (Answers, Guidance, Blessings)

Marriage (Answers, Guidance, Blessings)

Family (Answers, Guidance, Blessings)

Work (Answers, Guidance, Blessings)

Church (Answers, Guidance, Blessings)

Friends (Answers, Guidance, Blessings)

Community (Answers, Guidance, Blessings)

Enemies (Answers, Guidance, Blessings)

This is different than the goals and dreams prayers that you just prayed in the last exercise. This is very specific requests. It is okay. ASK!!!

Chapter #9
Spiritual Weapon of Alertness

One of the most forgotten spiritual weapons that God has given us is alertness. Right now, wherever you are, Satan is scheming to manipulate you and destroy the plan that God has for you. You must stay alert to how he is trying to do that to you. The Apostle Peter comes out boldly and states that we must be alert or we will be devoured.

> <u>Be of sober spirit, be on the alert.</u> *Your adversary, the devil, prowls around like a roaring lion, seeking someone to devour. But resist him, firm in your faith, knowing that the same experiences of suffering are being accomplished by your brethren who are in the world.* 1 Peter 5:8,9

Peter doesn't say, "You are protected; go into all the dens of evil in the world." No, he says you should be alert.

Alertness doesn't make the list of God's Armor in many books, but it should. It is crucial to defeating the Devil. In this chapter you will see how to utilize the two major forms of alertness that God has given us. The Devil's attack can come from different, unexpected places. We need to be ready. Don't be paranoid but be alert.

The list of spiritual heroes who stress the need for alertness is stunning. King David begins the Psalms with the statements: *How blessed is the man who does not walk in the counsel of the ungodly, nor stand in the path of sinners nor sit in the seat of the scoffers!* If we consistently listen to ungodly counsel, we will be lulled into thinking that wrong is right or God is not all that important. If we watch sinners do their sin, we are learning how to sin. Eventually we will begin to see sin as normal and as an option. If we hang out with cynics and pessimists, we will become accustomed to their point of view and tolerant of their skewed perspective. All of these three seemingly innocent activities keep us from being alert. We can become dull to the right choices and miss God's best for us.

Jesus tells us that He himself is alert about what is happening on His team. He knew that one of them was listening to and occasionally taking orders from the Devil. He was alert.

> *Jesus answered them, "Did I Myself not choose you, the twelve and <u>yet one of you is a devil?</u>" Now he meant Judas the son of Simon Iscariot, for he, one of the twelve, was going to betray Him.* John 6:70

Notice that Paul calls people to realize that the Devil wants us to believe that nothing will ever change and that Jesus is not coming back. We must be alert to what the Devil is doing and the fact that Judgment Day is coming.

> *Now as to the times and the epochs, brethren, you have no need of anything to be written to you. For you yourselves know full well that the day of the Lord will come just like a thief in the night. While they are saying, "Peace and safety!" then destruction will come upon them suddenly like labor pains upon a woman with child, and they will not escape. But you, brethren, are not in darkness, that the day would overtake you like a thief; for you are all sons of light and sons of day. We are not of night, nor of darkness; so then let us not sleep as*

Spiritual Weapon of Alertness

others do, <u>but let us be alert and sober</u>. For those who sleep do their sleeping at night, and those who get drunk get drunk at night. But since we are of the day, let us be sober, having put on the breastplate of faith and love, and as a helmet, the hope of salvation.
1 Thessalonians 5:1-5

In the spiritual battle we are waging to stay righteous, we must be of the day and have our eyes wide open. Put on the armor of light. Notice that God is telling us to not wander into a sinful or stupid manipulation of the Devil.

Love does no wrong to a neighbor; therefore love is the fulfillment of the law. Do this, knowing the time; that it is already the hour for you to awaken from sleep; for now salvation is nearer to us than when we believed. The night is almost gone, and the day is near. <u>Therefore let us lay aside the deeds of darkness and put on the armor of light.</u> Let us behave properly as in the day, not in carousing and drunkenness, not in sexual promiscuity and sensuality, not in strife and jealousy. But put on the Lord Jesus Christ, and make no provision for the flesh in regard to its lusts.
Romans 13:10-14

Notice how Peter says that some people have been entangled back in the sins of the past because they were not alert to the spiritual battle. They were causalities of war because of their lack of diligence and stupidity.

For if, after they have escaped the defilements of the world by the knowledge of the Lord and Savior Jesus Christ, they are again entangled in them and are overcome, the last state has become worse for them than the first. *For it would be better for them not to have known the way of righteousness, than having known it, to turn away from the holy commandment handed on to them. It has happened to them according to the true proverb, "A DOG RETURNS TO ITS OWN VOMIT," and, "A sow, after washing, returns to wallowing in the mire."* 2 Peter 2:20-22

God tells us in this next passage that many people will fall asleep at the switch and start listening to the teaching of demons. We must stay alert so we don't become prisoners of war.

But the Spirit explicitly says that in later times some will fall away from the faith, paying attention to deceitful spirits and doctrines of demons, by means of the hypocrisy of liars seared in their own conscience as with a branding iron, men who forbid marriage and advocate abstaining from foods which God has created to be gratefully shared in by those who believe and know the truth. For everything created by God is good, and nothing is to be rejected if it is received with gratitude; for it is sanctified by means of the word of God and prayer. 1 Timothy 4:1-4

Has the Devil defeated you in the past through anger? You should expect that he will try and work that scheme again. Has the Devil tempted you to be unfaithful to your marriage? Then find a way to be prepared for that temptation. Has the Devil deceived you through being gullible and too trusting of others? Then be alert and develop a way to keep that from happening again. We must be alert to the various ways that the Devil is trying to keep us from the abundant life God has planned for us (John 10:10).

Spiritual Weapon of Alertness

How can you put extra precautions and protections in place in the areas where you have already shown a weakness to giving in?

Let me help you see some of the ways he is coming after you. He may be tempting you to throw away your future for a mistress. He may be manipulating you through lies you are reading on the Internet. He may be oppressing you through fear by building a smaller and smaller box to live in because of your fears. He may be turning you away from the future you could have by getting you fixated on some unfair event from the past. He may be destroying your future through overindulgence in some pleasure. He may use others to convince you that you are worthless or insignificant, so you throw away your future through some foolish relationship, plan, or scheme.

Alertness is hidden at the end of the list of the Armor of God, but it should really be first in importance to many of us. Alertness is the early radar system that lets us realize what the Devil is doing. Alertness gives us time to prepare our resistance. Alertness allows us the ability to make the corrections in our thinking or living before the Devil exploits our weakness. Years ago, as a pastor, I had numerous people praying for God's protection for me and our church. On several occasions these prayer warriors warned me of what they sensed in prayer. One time they sensed that the Devil was going to try and compromise my integrity through my relationship with women at the church. I was single at the time so we (church leadership) took this information and designed a much more stringent protocol for any interaction with women at the church. Being alert to this potential threat gave us the time to thwart this scheme. Later we became aware of at least three women who had designs to compromise my integrity as a pastor but because of a alertness in prayer and church leadership, we sailed right through that time without ever having the scheme come to fruition.

We have to make sure that we do not fall asleep in the middle of Satan's manipulations. I had a friend who at one time helped rescue porn addicts recover from their addiction. He let his guard down and fell victim to adultery, destroying his marriage and his ministry. He was not alert.

Spiritual Workout

Who do you have in your life that will be brutally honest with you about where you are naïve, reckless, foolish, or deceived? Write down someone's name or go get someone who can fill this role.

Yes, it can happen to you, and you must have people who will be honest with you about what they see. The people who really love you probably don't tell you, but they already know.

I regularly ask my wife and other trusted men where am I limiting myself? Where do I have a blind spot I am not seeing? What do I need to change?

Spiritual Workout

Who is praying for you and can warn you of what they sense in prayer? Write down someone's name or go find people who will pray for you.

Alertness Exercises

There are two kinds of alertness systems God has given to us. These are warning systems: 1) Warnings that come from our life. We call this feedback. 2) Warning systems that protect us from known areas of weakness.

God is giving you feedback about your life

The following exercise will help you pay attention to the warning systems that God has already put in place in your life so that you won't fall victim to the Devil's lies and manipulations.

Throughout the Scriptures God tells that He is giving us feedback on whether our life is on course or off course. This feedback is called in the Bible reproof or rebuke. We call it feedback. Life is giving us feedback about how we are doing: When we are out of money before the end of month, that is feedback that something is wrong in our financial system; when our marriage is full of arguments and tension that is feedback that something is wrong with our marriage; when we are overweight and out of shape, it is feedback that something is wrong with our present nutrition and exercise plan. Of course we tend to ignore this kind of feedback because it suggests that we need to change something. Most of us have gotten used to ignoring the feedback in our life. We are paying a heavy price for our neglect of alertness.

Listen to Proverbs 1:22,23

> *How long, O naïve ones, will you love being simple-minded? And scoffers delight themselves in scoffing and fools hate knowledge? Turn to my **reproof (feedback)**, Behold I will pour out my spirit on you; I will make my words known to you.*

This verse tells us that when we ignore God's feedback, we are being naïve. But if we would pay attention to the feedback and make the needed correction, then things would get better and God's spirit would make us wiser.

Let me give you two examples. When I was a teenager I allowed a car that I was driving to run out of oil and go low on water. This caused the engine to be destroyed and the car to need a new engine. Because of this clear mistake that I made, my mom would always ask me every time I came home from college if I had checked the oil and water level. I resented her questions and felt like she did not need to do this just because of one mess-up in the past. But she never stopped, no matter how many times I asked her to stop. Then one time as I was coming home. I realized that my mom was going to ask that question, so I pulled off into a gas station and checked the oil and water so that I could say that I had checked it when she asked. It shocked her when I said that I had checked the oil and water level. And I did not get the lecture that I normally received about the need to check. The next two or three times I was coming home I also stopped and checked the oil and water level before I got home. My mother asked me those few times and when I said I had checked them, she completely stopped asking. This was a revelation to me. Once my mother realized that I could be trusted to actually check those things then her feedback stopped. I wanted the feedback to stop and had asked for it to stop, but it didn't stop until it got the responses it needed to stop. Sometimes in our lives we want the feedback to stop rather than doing what the feedback is suggesting.

A few years ago our family was having difficulties keeping up with all of the school and various expenses connected with our girls being in college. I kept trying to make the budgeting system work that we had used for twenty-plus years, but it wasn't working. I remember crying out to God to give me some direction on this because I was doing all that I knew to do and the feedback (the bank account) was telling me it wasn't enough. I needed some more knowledge and skills. I was amazed that just a few weeks after my prayer a man at church stopped me and thanked me for recommending a new budgeting software to his family. I had never heard of the software that he was thanking me for. He talked so glowingly about it that I felt I needed to check it out. I ended up purchasing it and it has completely fixed the problems that were not being addressed in our old budgeting system. The financial feedback I had been getting was telling me that I needed a new system and after praying about it, God gave me what I needed in a new system.

Too many people are getting feedback that says things are wrong, but because they don't know what to do or they don't want to go to the trouble of changing something, they get mad at the feedback. Don't do this. Feedback is just feedback. If the tree in the front yard is turning brown, it is feedback -- it is not the tree's fault. Listen to the feedback and make the changes that God is directing through the feedback.

Spiritual Workout

What feedback are you presently receiving in the relationships of life?

Let me run through the ten major relationships of life and have you take a look at some of the normal areas of feedback to see if any of these are happening in your life. If it is, then circle it and think through what you are going to do to pay attention to that feedback. Don't get mad at the feedback. Realize that God is trying to alert you to the fact that something needs to change.

God

Do your prayers seem to bounce off the ceiling instead of connecting to God and His help?

Is there a disconnect with you and God?

Do you feel guilty when you think of God?

Are you afraid to really let God control you life?

Are you angry at God?

What other feedback are you getting that suggests that this relationship could or should be different?

Spiritual Weapon of Alertness

Self : Body; Soul, and Spirit

Is your conscience bothering you?

Are you using and developing your area of creativity?

Do you feel like you have skills and abilities that you are not using or developing?

Do you have the education or degrees to get the job you really want?

Are you intrigued about learning something but you don't have the time or money?

Are you overweight?

Are you tired and lethargic a lot?

Do you have less energy than you used to?

What other feedback are you getting that suggests that this relationship could or should be different?

Marriage

Are there arguments and tension regularly in your marriage?

Do you not really want to spend time with your spouse?

Has the feelings of love, affection, and respect leaked away from your marriage?

Are you being blamed for things that happened to your spouse before your marriage?

Does your spouse just seem odd?

What other feedback are you getting that suggests that this relationship could or should be different?

Family

Do you not enjoy your children?

Would you rather be somewhere else than with your family?

Is there an elephant in the room with your family that no one wants to talk about it?

Are your children out of control?

When you ask other families to hang out, do they consistently decline?

What would have to change to make you or others want to be with your family?

What other feedback are you getting that suggests that this relationship could or should be different?

Work

Do you feel stuck at work?

Are you making less than you want to make?

Are you being passed over for promotions?

Is there more you could do, but they are not interested in your "extra" help?

Do the folks at work not regularly hang out with you?

Do you have friends at work?

Are you clear about what you are supposed to do at work?

What other feedback are you getting that suggests that this relationship could or should be different?

Finances

Do you run out money before the next paycheck comes in?

Are you overspending on some area consistently?

Are you making enough income to provide for your family or yourself?

Is the money all spent before you even get it?

Are you in debt?

Do you have an emergency fund?

Are you more financially prepared for life and retirement each year?

What other feedback are you getting that suggests that this relationship could or should be different?

Spiritual Weapon of Alertness

We need to pay attention when we are getting God's yellow alerts that something is wrong. Change course and move in a different way.

Dear Lord Jesus,

I want to live in the truth. Please help me be open to true feedback so that I can be set free. I realize that the Devil, my own flesh, and others have tried to keep me from knowing the truth, but I am ready. Please lovingly and powerfully show me the truth so that I live the life you planned for me. There are probably many areas where I have turned away from feedback. Show me at the proper time these truths that I have been missing so I can glorify you, Lord Jesus, in all that I do.

In Christ's Name,

Amen

Spiritual Workout

What warning systems need to be put in place for you to live a righteous, loving, and supremely successful life?

Are there particular issues or places or people that consistently bring out the worst in you or allow you to give into temptation? You may need to set up a warning system that will keep you away from those issues, out of those places, and away from those people. What are these weak spots in your life?

Issues that cause problems

Places that lead to trouble

People that regularly lead to destructive tendencies

Spiritual Workout

Three needs for warning systems

Years ago I discovered that the most successful people have the most warning systems in their life, not the least. The people with the most impact, influence, and relationships are usually the people with the most internal and external promptings telling them when they are on target and when they are off course. Therefore the more "successful" we are, the more warning systems we will have both internal and external and the more we will follow them. These open up the way to be more blessed and more successful. We can think that these are restricting, but they show us the narrow path to the blessed life. The Devil wants us to turn off all these warning systems and just live for the moment and just do what we feel, but he is trying to run our life in to a ditch.

Most of us need warning systems for three things.

1) What we should do but will forget

We need the warning systems to prod us into actions:

    Alarms, calendar, assistant, checklists, rules

    Birthdays, exercise, nutrition, social customs

Are there any of these warning systems that you need to pay attention to or put in place?

2) What we would do but shouldn't

The following is a small list of actions that different ones of us are tempted to do, and we would like to give into even though we know we shouldn't because it will damage others or ourselves. Circle or mark the actions that you have given in on and begin a process that will stop your involvement.

Gossip, look at porn, buy things we don't need, eat too much, talk about ourselves too much, be lazy, be critical or cynical, be greedy.

What other actions are you taking that you know you shouldn't but still do it? Write initials or some code so the material is left private.

In order to keep from doing these things, we usually need some form of accountability. This could be a person, a report, a software program, or any number of ways to bring us to a place where we won't give in to what we may want to do but know that we shouldn't.

Are there any of these areas where you know you shouldn't but you do not have adequate systems to keep you from doing it yet?

3) What will harm others but we are tempted to do?

These are those actions that will do significant damage to others for a few moments of pleasure for ourselves. In these areas we are self-focused and can easily forget the damage we will do to our lives because we are completely focused on what we want.

This might include: affairs, gambling, drugs, get-rich-quick schemes, witchcraft, fortune tellers, violence, vengeance, screaming, stealing, deceiving others, etc. Are there any other actions that you know are damaging to others and yourself but you have kept doing?

In order to keep from even going near these elements you may need very robust forms of warning systems if you are prone to giving in to these areas. You may need to determine how to stay away from these issues or situations entirely. You may have to have people ask you if you have moved in these directions daily, weekly, monthly. The key is that you are in charge of getting the right amount of warnings to you, so you don't harm others and destroy your future.

The proper warning systems for these weak areas are almost always routines, systems, phrases, approaches, fines, laws, and accountability. Put a plan in place with your accountability group so that you stay away from these problems.

Chapter 10
Building the Hedge of Protection

We are trying to build a spiritual hedge of protection around ourselves, our family, and eventually out as far as we can -- just as Job did.

> The LORD said to Satan, "Have you considered My servant Job? For there is no one like him on the earth, <u>a blameless and upright man, fearing God and turning away from evil.</u>" Then Satan answered the LORD, "Does Job fear God for nothing? <u>Have You not made a hedge about him and his house and all that he has, on every side?</u> You have blessed the work of his hands, and his possessions have increased in the land."
> Job 1:8-10

This will take the use of the various spiritual weaponry that God has provided through Christ: Resistance, Truth, Righteousness, The Gospel of Peace, Faith, Salvation, The Word of God, Prayer, and Alertness.

Spiritual Workout

1. Stand firm—Resistance: Practice taking no action, either mentally or physically, toward sin. If a sensual picture is available for viewing, take no action to look at it. If a person is flirting or being suggestive in some fashion, do not in any way signal with your eyes, face, mouth, hands, or body that you are interested. Temptation is often trying to get us to compromise in seemingly unimportant little ways. But stand firm even on the small things. Do not purchase the cable package that includes sensual material. Do not try and get around the Internet filter. Do not go to the sensual entertainment when you travel. Do not give into the get-rich-quick scheme. Do not purchase the impulsive desire. Do not say the negative or hateful thing.

2. Truth: Remind yourself again of the truth of the Christian Worldview. The ultimate reality in the universe is the Triune God. Above, beyond, and before anything, there is a Supreme Being we know of as God. He created the universe out of nothing and separate from Himself. He loved us enough to send His Son to pay the penalty for our selfishness and sin. He has communicated with us clearly and objectively without error in the Scriptures. He guides the Christian with His Holy Spirit. We can be forgiven of our sins and selfishness and have a right relationship with God through belief in Jesus Christ's life and death. Jesus Christ died, was buried, and rose from the dead. Mankind was created by God in His image but now is corrupted with a natural inclination toward selfishness and sin. God has called each Christian to join with other Christians to worship Him, to grow in understanding and Christian living, to evangelize others, to deeply connect with others, and to help the poor and afflicted. There is an afterlife where heaven and/or hell will be the final real destination of individuals. History will have an end when Jesus Christ returns a second time and breaks into human history as ruler and King.

3. Righteousness: Give thanks for the perfect life and death of Christ that allows God to establish a loving, accepting relationship with you. Eliminate anything you are doing that is clearly not righteous or pleasing to the Lord. Look for opportunities to meet the needs of others or benefit them in some way.

4. The Gospel of Peace: Re-embrace your acceptance of your absolute need of Christ's perfect life, death, and resurrection. It is Christ's work that has allowed you to be at peace with God and nothing can separate you from His loving relationship with you. Remind yourself that your relationship with God does not depend on you but on what Christ has already done. Because of what God has forgiven in you through Christ, stop fighting, hating, or criticizing others. Be at peace with others as far as it depends on you.

5. Faith: Commit again to trusting God's guidance, plans, lifestyle, and wisdom for your life. His way of life is a superior way of life for you. He is still in control. He can stop this difficult period whenever He wants. He loves you and will show you the way of escape. It is worthwhile to live God's way and trust Him.

6. Salvation: Force your mind to think again of what Christ has won for you through His life, death, and resurrection. Cry out to God for His way of escape from the schemes of Satan that you are facing. Ask God to see the way of escape He is providing when it comes. God chose you before the world began to receive His love and be in His family. You can relate to God directly because of the forgiveness of your sins. You are a member of God's forever family. God is working within you to make you more Christ-like. You have a home and citizenship in heaven. You are saved from facing the wrath of God. Christ is coming back for you. Heaven is where life will be revealed of which we only catch glimpses now. You have been given a guide for this life's path called the Holy Spirit. You find joy in purity instead of impurity. You have been forgiven. You will be given rewards for every Christ-like action you perform.

7. The Word of God: Recite Scripture that deals with the temptations and attacks that we are facing. Listen hard for the Scripture that God leads you to. Read appropriate sections of Scripture and be alert to God's highlighting of a particular Scripture. Slowly speak that particular Scripture over and over again under your breath, in your head, or out loud as you battle the tempting thought, the evil scheme, or the evil choice. Let your mind be filled with verses such as Colossians 3:16, Psalms 119:9-11, 1 Thessalonians 4:3-5, and 2 Timothy 2:22. Make little cards with these and other powerful Scriptures on them that you can carry with you all the time to refer to and read out loud when you face these times. Or put them on your phone so that you can refer to them quickly when they are needed.

8. Prayer: Ask God for strength to do the righteous thing instead of being sensual. Ask God to empower, bless, direct, or rebuke the people you know until the power of the temptation has passed. Keep praying for others until the power of the temptation is lessened and you can move on to other things.

9. Alertness: Ask God for spiritual alertness. Ask Him to send you friends, promptings, verses, books, or messages that will alert you to traps, schemes, and temptations that the Devil wants to use to destroy you. Develop a pattern of life that does not put you in the path of sinners or listening to the counsel of the ungodly. There are people, activities, situations, and circumstances that God is trying to have you avoid, but you have ignored Him in the past. Pay attention and avoid what He is saying to avoid. There are people, activities, situations, and circumstances that God is trying to have you move into, but you have been unwilling for some reason. Pay attention and move towards them.

Spiritual Workout
The most powerful use of each weapon right now in your life

Each of the pieces of the Armor of God are powerful weapons for building the life you want and that God has planned for you. In many cases the path to the life that is the best for you is blocked, or you are on the wrong path. These weapons when understood and used will reorient your life or get you unstuck or help you eliminate the destructive choices you are making now. Let's begin the process of using these weapons by praying through the list of weapons and asking God for just one answer.

What is the one use of this weapon that would make the most difference?

It may be that this use of a particular weapon is to move you in a positive direction, or it may be that the most powerful use of a particular weapon is to stop your progress in the wrong direction.

It may be that the most powerful use of a particular weapon is to expose how the Devil is manipulating you or lying to you.

Slowly pray through each spiritual weapon asking God to help you understand the one most powerful use of that weapon right now in your life. Write it down and ask God to guide you to the use of that weapon today and this next week. These spiritual weapons are supposed to be used. You will discover many ways to use these weapons in the weeks ahead, but this is a dynamic place to start.

Truth
What is the most powerful truth or use of truth for my life right now?

Righteous Actions
What is the most powerful righteous action I can do in my life right now?

Harmony /Peace Strategies
What is the most powerful peace or harmony strategy that I can use in my life right now?

Risk / Trust
What is the most righteous risk that I can take right now in my life?

Ways of Escape/ Deliverance
What righteous way of escape do I need to take right now in my life?

Biblical Words and Thoughts
What is the most powerful verse that I should be thinking about right now?

Answers to Prayer
What are the most important things I should be praying about right now?

Warning Systems
What is the most important warning that I should be paying attention to right now?

Chapter #11
Overview of the Armor of God

Remember that the Devil is about lies, fear, impulsiveness, evil (one person wins at another's expense), doubt, terror, meaningless activity, personal religion, condemnation, depression, anger, hatred, and so on. He wants you to act based upon lies, based upon fear, and based upon anger—so you have to keep yourself grounded. How do you guard your soul from the toxic infections of the Devil? Use the Armor of God as actual weapons protecting your soul (mind, will, emotions). No matter what you are thinking, feeling, or being offered, ask yourself the following questions and use the answers:

Spiritual Workout

Truth
What is the reality (truth) in your life right now?

What is the reality (truth) about God right now?

What is the reality (truth) about other people around you right now?

What truth do you need to know, feel, or do today to avoid doing evil?

Righteousness

Apply the righteousness of Christ to this feeling, this choice, this opportunity, this idea. What happens?

Can you imagine Christ doing this?

What would Christ do instead of doing this?

What is the righteous thing to do or not do right now?

What righteousness do you need to know, feel, or do today to avoid doing evil?

The Gospel of Peace

Apply the Gospel of Peace to this feeling, this possible choice, or this opportunity.

If God has really forgiven you, then how does it impact this feeling, this choice, or this opportunity?

What aspects of the Gospel of Peace do you need to know, feel, or do today to avoid doing evil?

Faith

Apply trusting God to this feeling, this choice, or this opportunity.

Does doing, saying, feeling this really line up with trusting God?

What elements of faith do you need to know, feel, or do today so you avoid evil?

Salvation

Apply salvation in Christ to this feeling, this choice, or this opportunity.

What escape routes has Christ given you to avoid this feeling, this choice, or this opportunity?

What elements of salvation do you need to know, feel, or do today?

The Word of God

Apply the Word of God to this feeling, this choice, or this opportunity.

Meditate on the Bible in your inner being. What is God saying?

What words from God do you need to pay attention to, memorize, feel, or do today to avoid doing evil?

Prayer
Ask God specifically about this feeling, this choice, or this opportunity.

What can you ask?

What can you use to counteract?

What can you think about instead?

What aspect of God's character can you worship in Him that will cover this distraction, temptation, or evil design?

What prayers do you need to pray today to avoid evil?

Alertness
Apply spiritual alertness to this feeling, this choice, or this opportunity.

What elements of alertness do you need to know, feel, or do today to avoid doing evil?

Conclusion

So what are we really saying to do when you are under spiritual attack? Use the Armor of God. Let me show you by a recent interaction I had on the phone. A lady called me and said that she was under demonic attack. She sensed the spirits around her in her home. She asked what she should do. I began going right down the pieces of the Armor for relief. **What truth does this woman need to know so that she can be free from this spiritual attack?**

I let her know that there were only three reasons that the demons would be there: 1) She did something. 2) Her ancestors did something. 3) Something was done in that place. I knew the family and so I thought that it was a case where her family had done something in the past, and the wicked spirits were making a claim on her life and future because of what her family had done in the past. I asked a prayer team member to pray for this young lady, and she said that when she asked the Lord about a familiar spirit, the Lord said, "No." We had already ruled out that something was done in that place. So that left us with the fact that she did something. I asked her what the attack felt like. She said it was all about fear. She said she had felt this off and on for years. She had as an eight-year old girl given into fear in a big way and never really got over it.

I gave her some truth about fear that comes from the recovery world. They describe F.E.A.R. as Fantasized Exaggerations Appearing Real. We talked for some time about the fact that fear's power is that it can exaggerate the worst possible scenario and make it seem like it is about to happen. But it is always an imaginary enemy. If you are afraid in this way, then it is always an exaggeration. In her case she was still embracing the exaggerations of an eight-year old girl. The truth about her fears was that they were not real, but they still held great power in her life.

Next I asked myself **what righteous action could this young lady do that would thwart this spiritual attack?** I suggested that this young lady and her husband anoint their new house with oil and dedicate it to the Lord Jesus Christ for His use. This brought her husband into the battle and connected them together. It also formally dedicated them, their marriage, and their home to the Lord. It was very helpful. Without righteous actions, the afflicted person is not claiming their victory in Christ. Too many people want to be rid of the demons and spiritual attacks, but they do not want to take any steps of action themselves. Thankfully that was not the case with this young lady.

As I was talking to the young lady, I asked myself **what actions of peace and harmony could this young lady do to cut down this spiritual attack?** She and her husband happened to have her parents over at the house, and the parents had had some strained relationships with the new couple in the past. I asked her husband and her father to take a strong position of leadership in dedicating the house but also in praying for this young lady. After the family prayed for the house and for each other, the father was just glowing with how this was bringing the families together. Everyone was on the same side of the line, fighting a common enemy together. Their united prayer time and conversation really pushed back the darkness.

Then I asked myself **what God-ordained risks could be taken that would push back this spirit of fear in this young lady's life?** It seemed obvious that one of the keys was to have her husband take a stronger protector role. So I asked him to lead in prayer. Even though he had not been a Christian all that long

Conclusion

nor was he familiar with strong spiritual warfare, he jumped right in and began praying strong prayers for his wife as I led him. This was a risk to ask this relatively new believer to step up and confront a spirit of fear that was plaguing his wife, but it seemed like the right risk and it paid off handsomely. He grew. She felt protected. The spirit of fear was attacked from another angle. He knew what his wife was going through. This episode and his leadership drew them together as a couple.

As we continued through the time, I asked myself **what God-ordained way of escape is going to help this young lady?** After we had prayed and pushed through the fear initially and she was feeling fine, she mentioned that she was really concerned (read afraid) about the fact that her husband was going to be away on business the next week. She did not want to be alone. Near the end of our time on the phone, I circled back to this issue and the solution that I thought God presented. Since her mom was sitting near her and her mom understood more about spiritual warfare than she did, I suggested that she plan on going to be with her mom during the week that her husband was away rather than stay in the empty house. She would be less susceptible to fear, she and her mom would connect deeply on things that mattered, and she would be able to grow in her faith with her mom. All this would drive the spirit of fear away from her more thoroughly.

I know that at some point God is going to whisper a verse of Scripture to me or to the afflicted person, **so I wait for what Scripture verse will God whisper so that I can quote it out loud and drive back the person and work of the Devil.** While I was talking to the young lady, and shortly after I found out that the major attack was a spirit of fear, the Lord prompted me with the verse in 1 John 4:18, *There is no fear in love; but perfect love casts out fear, because fear involves punishment, and the one who fears is not perfected in love.* I quoted the verse out loud to her and repeated it several times after the Lord whispered it to me. I also directed her to look up the verse, read it over and over, and say it over and over until it was memorized.

It is always clear that God is going to have me pray during any session that we are trying to help someone who is battling a spiritual attack. This was no different but **I needed to stay alert to what kind of prayer was needed, what should I pray about, who should I be praying for, and when should we pray.** We prayed at numerous points through the time: we prayed at the beginning; we prayed when we thought it was about an ancestral curse; we prayed when we discovered it was about her fear; we prayed for their house; I had her husband pray; I had her father pray; I had her pray. After they anointed their house dedicating it to the Lord, I had them pray a prayer dedicating her and her husband to the Lord. This wonderful time of prayer was what her father commented on that was helping bond the family together. It really pushed back the darkness and attacks of fear.

Finally, whenever spiritual attacks are encountered and rebuffed, there is a need for evaluation. I asked myself the question **what precautions need to be put into place so that this spiritual attack will not succeed in the future?** I told the husband that I would send him prayers that he could pray over his family every night to protect his wife and himself from spiritual attack. I also told the young lady about a spiritual gift that she seemed to be displaying in the midst of the time that evening that needed to be developed. I also suggested that more time of praying together with the father and the mother, as well as between husband and wife, would go a long way to protecting the young lady from these kinds of spiritual attacks.

This is how the Armor of God works in a practical way. God has truth that will disintegrate the schemes of the Devil. God has righteous actions that will move you away from sinful

Conclusion

temptations and destructive urges. God has peace moves and harmony strategies that will push back the wickedness that wants to invade our lives. God has risks that He wants us to take that will completely change the ability of the enemy to attack us. God has ways of escape from the traps of the Devil that we should take. God whispers the scriptures to us so we can thrust it into the face of the situation and the Devil and defeat him. God draws us to prayer so that we can ask for help, receive wisdom, increase power for others, and/or change the nature of the battle. God also is warning us about future attacks and asking that we prepare for future attacks. Put on the Armor of God and become protected and able to make an impact for God because you are defeating the Devil and his schemes.

Each week we face lies, fear, doubt, frustration, temptation, and depression that is designed to derail, distort, or destroy our future. The questions that I am hoping you will be asking after reading this book and doing the exercises are:

How do I bring new truth into these thoughts or opportunities?

How do I bring new righteousness into this situation?

How do I inject new levels of the forgiveness and peace of God into my relationships?

How do I re-embrace my trust in who God is, what He has said, and the righteous path I know I should be on?

How do I stay alert for God's ways of escape even as I understand and utilize God's amazing salvation and its work on and in me as I head to heaven?

How do I fill my mind with Scripture, listening for the Holy Spirit's bringing it to mind at just the right moment?

How do I interact with God in more ways so His guidance, wisdom, comfort, steadfastness, and holiness are more a part of my life?

How do I stay alert to the ways the Devil is lying, manipulating, and tempting me so I won't miss God's best for me?

God has given the Christian the means to protect ourselves, our family, our communities, and even our nation from the manipulations of the Devil. But we must know how to use the spiritual weapons He gives us (Ephesians 6:10-18). He uses multiple illustrations to help us understand what these spiritual weapons are: a hedge, armor, light shining in a dark place, invisible power, etc. But the spiritual weapons themselves are always the same throughout the Scriptures: Truth, Righteousness, Peace, Faith, Salvation, the Word of God, Prayer, and Alertness. Each of the weapons comes from God, and yet the believer must use each weapon in very practical ways or they will be of no use. It is time that we don't just study these weapons, but we become practiced at using them.

Spiritual Workout

What would happen if you made sure that you were receiving and giving truth?

What would happen if you made sure that all your actions flowed from a righteous desire to benefit everyone, not just yourself?

Conclusion

What would happen if you really did whatever was needed to live in harmony with the people in your life?

What would happen if you trusted God and His way in every area of your life and pushed through the changes needed to live God's way in every relationship?

What would happen if you stayed alert to God's escape routes instead of giving into temptation and/or allowed God to more fully bring your salvation out through your life?

What would happen if you started thinking through solutions in your life biblically?

What would happen if you interacted with God about everything and waited for his answers?

What would happen if you were willing to let God show you how the Devil is right now scheming against you?

God has given you all you need to be free from the lies, fear, anger, manipulations, and temptations of the Devil. Pick up the spiritual weapons in the Armor of God and begin to live the life you were meant to live. Let me state the obvious: You can't ask someone else to do your push-ups for you. In the same way, you can't expect others to carry and use the weapons of the spirit for you. You have to pick them up and you have to use them.

How to Use This Book

There are five ways that this material was designed for use. Originally it was to be used as an Intensive Discipleship material for small groups of men or women to help them move significantly forward in their Christian life. It can also be used for a personal devotion, mentor-directed study, a class format, or a sermon series with small groups. I have outlined how this could be conducted.

Small Group Study

1. Ask three to five people to join you in doing this study. Participate in a small groups program within your church in which people are assigned to your small group to cover this material or develop your own group.

2. Set aside an hour to an hour-and-a-half each week (or each month) to do the three crucial things required for spiritual life-change. First, discuss what happened when you practiced the spiritual exercises in the previous lesson. Second, learn about the next set of exercises and information. Third, take personal prayer requests from each member. This can often be the most effective if it is done at breakfast or lunch in a restaurant before or during the workday. It doesn't have to be at church. In fact, many times it is better if it is not.

3. The time should be divided into three sections.

    a. The first 20-30 minutes should be spent sharing what happened when each person practiced the spiritual exercises that were assigned. Everyone must share even if they do not think that they were successful.

b. The second 10-30 minutes are spent in learning the next week or month's lessons and exercises.

c. The final 10-30 minutes are spent taking prayer requests from everyone. The prayer requests must be about the person themselves. This is not the time to have the group pray for a family member.

4. Each member of the group can read the book for further understanding of the information and exercises. The time spent together is not primarily a presentation time.

5. If one or more of the people have not tried or mastered the exercises, then the leader should feel free to repeat the same lesson again and again until this spiritual exercise is mastered.

6. If the group is meeting monthly rather than weekly, then more exercises are assigned. It can be helpful to have some form of accountability set up to make sure people are working on the exercises. This may be a daily or weekly e-mail stating what exercise they tried. The full explanation will come in the group time; but if everybody e-mails or texts what they are doing, then everybody stays on track.

Let's take a look at the first small group meeting:

1. Let everyone introduce himself or herself. A 60-second bio is usually helpful and lets everyone get to know everyone else.

2. Open in prayer.

3. Introduce the topic that you will be exploring and pass out the books. Give an overview of the whole series.

4. Explain the first week or month's exercises.

5. Save 10-20 minutes for personal prayer requests.

How to Use This Book

The key to an effective discipleship group is not what the teacher says; it is what the disciple does. So give each person lots of time to tell about what happened when he or she started to practice the discipline. If the people in the group did not adequately try the discipline or did not see results from trying the discipline, then spend another week on that discipline. The goal of the group is not to get through the material within a specific amount of time but to develop new spiritual habits that will change their lives.

Personal Devotional Study

A second way to use this material is as a personal devotional study. In this format you can work through the material and look up the verses on your own, taking notes, practicing the exercises, and writing down your experiences for personal review. In this type of study, proceed at your own pace. It may be one chapter a week, or it may be one chapter a day. The key is that the information is digested and the exercises are tried until some level of mastery is accomplished. It can be helpful to share your progress in this material with a mentor or spiritual accountability partner.

Let's take a look at what a personal devotional study would look like:

1. Open in prayer.
2. Read the material in the chapter.
3. Practice the exercise(s) suggested.
4. Record what you did, what happened when you did it, and what you continue to do because of using this exercise.
5. Practice the exercise again or in a different way until mastered.

Mentor-Directed Study

One of the most powerful ways of using this material is to ask a respected Christian you know to mentor you through this material. They do not need to do the study with you, but they do need to monitor and encourage you in the process of this study.

1. Ask a mentor to listen to your progress through this material once a month and pray for you as you explore these issues and exercises.

2. Meet the first time with your mentor and purchase a book for them so they can be tracking your progress. This meeting could be at a restaurant or a coffee house so that the meeting is more informal.

    a. Let them know what you are hoping to accomplish with this study and at what speed you would like to move through the material.

    b. Give them the freedom to teach, correct, rebuke, and train you as you move through the material (2 Timothy 3:16).

    c. Agree to meet monthly or weekly to hear updates on how you are doing. Remember, this is about you and not about them. They are mentoring you through this material and may not be going through it themselves. They are your spiritual guide, not a co-laborer.

    d. Have your mentor watch you pray or practice the exercise as they watch. They may be able to suggest ways to more effectively practice the spiritual exercise.

How to Use This Book

3. Ask your mentor to follow the following format for your monthly or weekly sessions:

   a. Spend 20-30 minutes listening to what you have done and experienced as you have worked through the exercises.

   b. Listen to their insights and additions.

   c. Spend 10-20 minutes of their assigning and exploring the next chapter or reassigning the current material because they think there is a need to dwell on these ideas or habits more thoroughly.

   d. Spend 10-20 minutes giving the mentor three specific personal prayer requests you would like them to pray for until the next meeting.

4. Realize that your mentor may want to move off in tangents that are not directly tied to the material in this study guide, but that is what you want. They have life experience and spiritual wisdom that you want to be poured into your life. A mentor can often see mistakes or missteps that are about to take place when we cannot see them. Also, mentors can listen for the emotional, psychological, or spiritual pain that we have not been able to talk about before.

Class Format

A fourth way to use this material is in a class or mid-week teaching time at the church. The material that is contained in the book can be presented to a class, but it should take only about half the time allowed for the class. The other half of the time should be used for small groups to discuss what happened the week before when the discipline was tried. Also allow for questions and prayer requests in regard to a growing spiritual life. This material should be repeated regularly as a part of a church's ongoing discipleship strategy. Every year, or every other year, a church can run one of these classes so that people are moving forward.

The greatest danger to using this material in a class setting is that the teacher will use the whole time to present the material, not allowing adequate discussion of what happened when it was tried.

Second, there is the danger that it will be offered as new information only, rather than as new practices or habits to incorporate into their life. The value of this material is in the exercises, not in the information. It is not possible to have a consistently deep walk with God without some of these disciplines being a part of their life. These materials are not just for delivering new information; they are to be practiced.

A third danger in using this material in a classroom setting is that the teacher or facilitator may not feel the freedom to repeat a discipline until all in the class have adequately tried it. There needs to be the freedom to go back over material that is not fully embraced until it has been adequately explored.

How to Use This Book

Let's take a look at what using this material in a classroom setting would look like.

Advertise the class in various places at church, work, or community. For the first classroom period, let's take a look at what the first meeting of the classroom setting would look like:

1. Open in prayer.
2. Introduce an overview of the topic and pass out the books.
3. Let people know that this is an exercise / application-focused group, not a new information-focused group. They will learn new information but only so that they can then apply it to their life.
4. Introduce the first few exercises that will be tried in the first week or month.
5. Break the group into small groups for personal prayer requests.

For the remaining class periods, the following is the format for the standard meeting:

1. Open in prayer.
2. Give people 10-30 minutes to break into small groups of three or four and tell each other how the exercises from the last meeting went.
3. Spend 10-30 minutes explaining the new concepts and exercises to the group.
4. Put the group back into their small groups for personal prayer requests. Everybody has to share something that they want everyone to pray about.

Sermon Series and Small Groups

A fifth way to use this material is as a sermon series with accompanying small groups. This is where the whole church listens to the sermon series that the pastor is preaching, and then all small groups practice the material by doing the spiritual workouts at the end of each chapter. This is really a lab-lecture model of discipleship. It can be quite effective if the small group allows people to talk about trying the various disciplines. This is a way to jump-start Sunday morning attenders into people who are serious about developing spiritual habits. This multi-pronged approach can be very effective if there is adequate planning and opportunity for new groups to form even after the sermon series has started.

The goal of this book is that many Christians will begin practicing their Christianity and experiencing new levels of closeness with God. The process of walking with Christ takes time. The addition of new habits of life is essential. Expect that some will try these disciplines and then stop. Expect that others will have been waiting for this material for a long time and can quickly push to new depths with God. Patiently persevere. You and others will reap great joy in the presence of God.

About the Author

Dr. Gil Stieglitz is an author, speaker, catalyst, professor, leadership consultant, and President/Founder of Principles to Live By. He is currently Executive Pastor of Adventure Christian Church in Roseville, California, an adjunct professor at Western Seminary (Sacramento Campus), and a church consultant for Thriving Churches International. He is also on the board at Courage Worldwide – a wonderful organization that rescues children forced into sexual slavery. He has been a denominational executive for fifteen years with the Evangelical Free Church of America. He was senior pastor at a church in southern California for seventeen years.

Other Resources by Gil Stieglitz

Books
Becoming Courageous
Breakfast with Solomon Volume 1
Breakfast with Solomon Volume 2
Breakfast with Solomon Volume 3
Breaking Satanic Bondage
Deep Happiness: The Eight Secrets
Delighting in God
Delighting in Jesus
Developing a Christian Worldview
God's Radical Plan for Husbands
God's Radical Plan for Wives
Going Deep In Prayer: 40 Days of In-Depth Prayer
Leading a Thriving Ministry
Marital Intelligence
Mission Possible: Winning the Battle Over Temptation
Spiritual Disciplines of a C.H.R.I.S.T.I.A.N
They Laughed When I Wrote Another Book About Prayer, Then They Read It
Touching the Face of God: 40 Days of Adoring God
Weapons of Righteousness Study Guides
Why There Has to Be a Hell

If you would be interested in having Gil Stieglitz
speak to your group, you can contact him
through the website
www.ptlb.com